Babies Names

Babies Names

Amber Grayson

A Siena Book
Siena is an imprint of Parragon Book Service Ltd

This edition first published by
Parragon Book Service Ltd in 1996

Parragon Book Service
Unit 13-17
Avonbridge Trading Estate
Atlantic Road
Avonmouth
Bristol BS11 9QD

Produced by Magpie Books Ltd, London

ISBN 0 75251 434 2

A copy of the British Library Cataloguing in Publication Data is available from the British Library.

Printed and bound in Great Britain by
BPC Paperbacks Ltd
A member of
The British Printing Company Ltd

Introduction

How do you go about choosing a name for your new baby? Your partner likes **Timothy** but it reminds you of the horrible boy you sat next to at school and you both thought **Claire** was the one, until you remembered it was the name of his ex.

How do you decide what to call this new person, when you don't know exactly what he/she will look like. Although you can probably guess that he/she will have grandpa's hair and a yell like Shirley Bassey, you can't be absolutely certain about the rest of it. How many times have you heard, 'He doesn't look like a **Piers/Guy/David** . . .'? What if you name her **Bella** or **Bonita** and she ends up looking like Medusa, or if you choose **Blake** or **Rory** and he turns out to be mousey?

If you choose 'old' **Aldous** or 'married' **Beulah** you're obviously not playing by the rules but if you pick 'bald' **Calvin** you're probably going to be spot on – at least for a year or so. Likewise if you decide on 'raging' **Deirdre**. But if you call her **Cher** or **Cara**, will she end up costing you a fortune.

And what about personality? How do you know that cute, little **Tabitha** won't grow up to be a truck driver, or chubby **Burt** a ballet dancer? If 'starry' **Estelle** is your choice, it doesn't follow that she'll end up on the stage or screen, or that 'victorious' **Eunice** and 'champion' **Neil** will always win all the prizes.

You want to be different, but is it fair to lumber your child with a name that makes him/her stand out from the crowd just that little too far – perhaps a case of Small Poppy Syndrome? At the same time, you probably don't want several strange children sharing your sandwiches every time you call your **Sophie** over to the picnic blanket.

You want a name that won't be dated by the time he/she is an adult, but don't want to choose one that sounds too modern and might be just a flash in the pan. Until recently **Florence, Lily** and **Emily** were considered old ladies' names, but now they're all the rage. Conversely a name like **Louise** which has remained moderately popular in this country, is considered in France to be down there with the Ediths and Gertrudes You can pick a name that's old-fashioned and unpopular now in the hope that it will come round again as **Herbert** is growing up, but what happens if it doesn't?

What if your daughter takes her husband's surname when she marries, and finds herself known as Annette Curtins or Eileen Dover for the rest of her life? And how can you be sure that at some point in your child's life, his/her name, or its diminutive, won't become a new slang word? When Mr and Mrs Head named their son **Richard**, how were they to know they would be making him a laughing stock?

How can you prevent a car company from naming their latest hatchback after him, or more likely, her. Or that **Harriet** and **Isabel** won't become consumable trademark names like Lillet and Flora?

You can't, of course, but there are some precautions you can take to ensure that your child won't hate its name, or you, for the rest of its life.

- Pick two names (or more) so that your child will have a choice in later life. Some parents prefer to use a family name (eg. grandmother/father's) as the second name.
- Say the names out loud together with the surname.

Names that flow together are easier to say and always sound better (think how many times it's necessary to repeat your own name aloud).

- Work our the diminutives and any possible nick-names that could be derived from the name, and see how they sound with the surname.
- How do the names sound with those of the other siblings? Brothers **Thomas** and **Jeremy/Gerald** might seem fine in full, but how about Tom and Jerry? The same goes for **William** and **Benjamin**. Remember the Flower Pot Men?
- Make sure the initials of the first name, together with the surname, don't form an acronym, so that you avoid such things as fatty Freda Alice Thompson or nobby Nicholas Owen Brown.

Once you've made your choice in ignorant bliss, you can watch them grow up and prove you wrong. 'Manly' **Andrew** disappears inside his Baby-Gro every time someone comes near his pram and 'delicate' **Delilah** has taken up body building. Perhaps you could shorten her name to Del . . . Girl?

Nova unfortunately won't be new forever and **Omega** wasn't the last of the brood after all. **Fidel** and **Fidelia** aren't as faithful as you'd hoped and **Simon**'s nose isn't as small as you thought it would be. And how is it that **Verity** tells fibs and **Felix** and **Joy** are as miserable as sin, whilst 'industrious' **Amelia** does nothing all day and **Amos** won't give you a hand with the shopping (didn't his name mean 'he who carries')? If **Perdita** wants to become a navigator and **Philip**'s terrified of horses then isn't it all rather telling?

So whilst you're about it, why not look up your own name? You might be surprised to discover what expectations your parents had of you!

A

Aaron (m)
Hebrew, originally from Arab *Haroun*, meaning 'mountaineer' or 'inspired enlightener'.
Variants Aron, Arran, Arron.
Famous name Aaron Copland, twentieth-century composer and musician.

Abel (m)
Biblical name of the younger son of Adam and Eve, who was murdered by his brother Cain out of jealousy (Genesis IV:1–8). Briefly popular with the Puritans in the seventeenth century, but otherwise this name has never been much used.

Abigail (f)
Hebrew, meaning 'exaltation of my father' or 'source of joy'.
Diminutives Abi, Abby, Abbie.
Variant Abagail.
This name was often used to refer to a young lady's maid, perhaps because in the Bible Abigail was one of King David's wives, who refers to herself as 'thy servant'.

Abner (m)
Not often used in Britain, but quite popular in the USA. A biblical name meaning 'father of light' in Hebrew.
Variant Avner (Jewish).

Abraham (m)
Hebrew, meaning 'father of a multitude'.
Diminutive Abe.
Variant Abram.

Ada (f)
The first recorded use of this name is a seventh-century abbess in France, but it is thought to be English, though of uncertain origin – possibly a shortened form of Adelaide or a version of the biblical Adan meaning 'happy' (borne by the wives of Lamech and Esau, in Genesis). It became popular in the Regency era – Lord Byron's daughter by Anne Isabella Milbanke was named Ada – and throughout the nineteenth century, but is rare nowadays.

Adam (m)
Hebrew, meaning 'red earth' or 'earth man'.
Feminine Adamina.
Famous name Adam Faith, the popular singer, actor and producer.

Adelaide (f)
Old German, meaning 'of noble rank, a princess'.
Variants Ada, Adalaide, Adele, Adela, Adeline, Adelina, Adell, Heidi, Alice, Alina.
Famous name Adelina Patti, world famous Victorian soprano.

Adolf (m)
Old Teutonic, meaning 'noble wolf' or 'noble hero'.
Variant Adolphus.
Famous (or rather infamous) name Adolf Hitler, German dictator and instigator of the Second World War, for which reason it is rarely used today.

Adrian (m)
Latin from the place name (Adria, N. Italy).
Variant Hadrian.
Feminine Adria, Adriana, Adrianne, Adrien, Adrienne.
Famous name Adrian Moorhouse, swimmer.

Agatha (f)
Greek, meaning 'good'.
Variant Agathe.
Diminutive Aggie (see also Agnes).
Famous names Saint Agatha, a third-century Sicilian martyr whose feast day is celebrated on 5 February; Agatha Christie, famous English detective novelist.

Agnes (f)
Greek, meaning 'chaste, pure'.
Variants Senga (reversed form), Agnese, Agness, Agneta, Agnetta, Annice, Annis, Inez (Spanish), Ines (Italian).
Diminutives Aggie (see also Agatha), Nessie, Nesta, Agna, Neta.
Famous names Saint Agnes, patron saint of young virgins, martyred *c.* 304 at the age of thirteen. Her feast day is on 21 January, on the eve of which you may dream of your future husband. John Keats wrote a famous poem 'St Agnes's Eve'; Agnes de Mille, daughter of Cecil B. de Mille was a distinguished American choreographer.

Aidan (m)
Gaelic, meaning 'fire'.
Variants Aiden, Adin.
Famous name Saint Aidan was a monk of Iona sent by King Oswald to Northumbria. He established a monastery on the island of Lindisfarne. This name has become quite popular over the last forty years.

Aileen (f)
See Eileen.

Ainslie (m,f)
Surname and place name of uncertain origin.
Variant Ainsley.

Aisha (f)
Arabic, meaning 'woman'.
Variants Ayesha, Aesha, Aiesha, Ieasha, Yiesha.
Famous name In Rider Haggard's novel *She*, Ayesha was 'she who must be obeyed'.

Alan (m)
Late Latin, meaning 'harmony', later a Celtic name.
Variants Allen, Allan, Alun, Alain (French), Alyn, Allin, Allon.
Feminine Alana, Alaine, Alena, Alina, Allana, Allena, Alayne, Alayna.
Famous names Alan Bates, actor; Alana Hamilton (ex-wife of George Hamilton and of Rod Stewart).

Alasdair (m)
Gaelic form of Alexander.
Variants Alisdair, Alastair, Alistair, Allister, Alaister, Alistaire, Alyster.
Diminutives Al, Allie, Ally.
Famous name Alistair Maclean, popular British novelist.

Alban (m)
Latin from the place, Alba, meaning 'white hill'.
Variant Albany.

Albert (m)
Norman, meaning 'noble and bright'.
Feminine Alberta, Albertina, Albertine.
Diminutives Bert, Bertie.
Famous names Albert the Great, a famous Dominican scholastic philosopher; Prince Albert, consort of Queen Victoria, after whom an albert, a type of watchchain he wore, was named; Albert Schweitzer, musician and medical missionary; Albert Einstein, the greatest physicist of all time.

Aldous (m)
German, meaning 'old'.
Variant Aldo.
Famous name Aldous Huxley, English novelist and author of *Brave New World* (1932).

Alec (m)
Diminutive of Alexander, used independently.
Variants Alex, Alic, Alick, Aleck.
Diminutives Lec, Lex.
Famous name Alec Stewart, English Test cricketer.

Alexander (m)
Greek, meaning 'defender of men'.
Diminutives Alex, Alec, Alick, Sandy, Sander.
Famous names Alexander the Great, King of Macedon; Alexandre Dumas, French novelist and playwright; Alexander Graham Bell, inventor of the telephone; Alexander Solzhenitsyn, Soviet novelist expelled from

USSR in 1974; Alexander Calder, twentieth-century artist famous for his mobiles.

Alexandra (f)
Feminine form of Alexander.
Variants Alessandra, Alexandria, Alexandrina, Alexina, Alexia, Cassandra.
Diminutives Sandie, Sandra, Zandra.
Famous names Queen Alexandra, wife of Edward VII; Zandra Rhodes, fashion designer.

Alexis (m,f)
Greek, meaning 'helper'.
Famous name Alexis was the character played by Joan Collins in the soap *Dynasty*.

Alfred (m)
Old English, meaning 'elf counsel'.
Feminine Alfreda.
Famous names Alfred the Great, ninth-century King of Wessex; Sir Alfred Hitchcock, film director known for his suspense films; Alfred Munnings, English painter of horses; Alfred Deller, English counter-tenor.

Algernon (m)
Old French, meaning 'bewhiskered'.
Famous name Algernon Swinburne, impressive, and notorious, Victorian poet.

Alice (f)
Greek, meaning 'truth, nobility'.
Variants Alicia, Alysia, Alyssa, Alisha, Alissa, Alison, Alisa, Alix, Alys, Elke (German).
Diminutives Al, Allie, Ally.
Famous names Lewis Carroll's famous novel *Alice's Adventures in Wonderland*, whose heroine was named

after Alice Liddell; Alice Cooper (m), rock vocalist and composer.

Alina (f)
English and French, possibly a variant of Adeline or Aileen, first used in the Middle Ages. Its renewed popularity may be partly due to its resemblance to the Gaelic word for 'lovely' (*alainn*).
Variant Aline.

Alison (f)
Gaelic, meaning 'famous war'.
Variants Allison, Allyson, Alyson, Alisoun, Alysoun, Alisanne, Alysanne.
Diminutives See those for Alice above.
Famous names Alison Lurie, American satirical novelist; Alison Steadman, British actress.

Allegra (f)
Latin, meaning 'cheerful, jaunty'.
Famous name First used as a name by Byron and Claire Clairmont, for their illegitimate daughter.

Alma (f)
Italian, meaning 'soul, spirit'.
The English name that became fashionable in the last century after the Battle of Alma (1854) in the Crimea.
Famous names In Edmund Spenser's epic poem, *The Faerie Queene*, Alma typifies the soul; Alma Cogan, popular singer.

Althea (f)
Greek, meaning 'to heal'.
Possibly a corruption of Althaea of Greek legend. In medieval times Althea was the name given to the mallow plant.

Alvin (m)
Old English, meaning 'noble friend'.
Variants Aylwyn, Alwyn.
Feminine Alvina, Alvena, Alwyne, Alwyna.
Diminutive Alvie (m,f).
Famous name Alvin Stardust, British pop singer.

Amabel (f)
Old French, meaning 'lovable'.
This name was once very popular but is hardly used nowadays. It is probably the origin of both Annabel and Mabel.

Amanda (f)
Latin, meaning 'deserving of love'.
Masculine Amand.
Diminutives Manda, Mandi, Mandy.

Amber (f)
Arabic, meaning 'ambergris'.
First used at the end of the nineteenth century, its modern popularity may be due to the very successful popular novel by Kathleen Windsor, *Forever Amber*.
Variant Ambretta.

Ambrose (m)
Greek, meaning 'immortal, divine'.
Variant Emrys (Welsh).
Feminine Ambrosine, Ambrosina.
Famous names Saint Ambrose, fourth century bishop of Milan, celebrated for his organization of church music. His feast day is 7 December and his emblems are a beehive and a scourge; Ambrose Bierce, American writer, whose best-known work is *The Devil's Dictionary*.

Amelia (f)
Latin, meaning 'industrious'.
Variant Amalia (Italian).
Famous name Amelia Earhart (1898–1937), the first woman to fly solo across the Atlantic.

Amos (m)
Hebrew, meaning 'strong, courageous, burden-bearer'.
Famous name Amos Oz, Israeli novelist.

Amy (f)
Old French, meaning 'loved'.
Variants Aimée (French), Ame, Amata (Italian), Amia, Amey, Amie.
Masculine Amatus, Amato.

Anaïs (f)
From the Russian 'Ana' meaning 'she'.
Famous name Anaïs Nin, diarist and erotic writer, much admired by Madonna.

Anastasia (f)
Greek, meaning 'resurrection'.
Variant Anastatia.
Diminutives Stacy, Stacey, Stacie.
Famous name Anastasia, daughter of Tsar Nicholas II, believed by some to have survived her family's assassination.

Andrea (f)
See Andrew.

Andrew (m)
Greek, meaning 'manly, warrior'.
Variants Anders (Scandinavian), André (French), Andreas (Greek).
Feminine Andra, Andrea (a boy's name in Italy),

Andrée, Andrene, Andrena, Andreana, Andrewina, Andrette, Drena, Andrina, Andrietta.
Diminutives Andy, Andie, Drew.
Famous names St Andrew, patron saint of Scotland, Greece and Russia, whose feast day falls on 30 November; Andrew Maxwell, American celebrated poet; Andrew Carnegie, millionaire who provided public libraries in Britain and the USA.

Anita (f)
Originally the Spanish diminutive of Ana (Anne), this name is now popular in most English-speaking countries.
Famous name Anita Ekberg, actress.

Aneurin (m)
Welsh, meaning 'honour'.
Variant Aneirin.
Diminutive Nye.
Famous name Aneurin Bevan, first administrator of the National Health Service.

Angela (f)
Greek, meaning 'messenger'.
Variants Angelica, Angelina, Angeline, Angelique, Angelita.
Masculine Angel (also feminine), Angelo.
Diminutives Angie, Angy.

Angharad (f)
Welsh, meaning 'beloved'.
Famous name Angharad Rees, actress.

Angus (m)
Gaelic, meaning 'one choice'.
Feminine Angusina.

Ann (f)
Form of Hannah, Hebrew meaning 'grace'.
Variants Anne, Anna, Annette, Anita, Anika, Anneka, Anouska, Anya, Nancy, Nanette.
Diminutives Annie, Anny, Netta, Netty (Annette).
Combinations of Ann with other names – Annamarie, Annemarie, Annalisa, Anneliese.
Famous names Anne Boleyn and Anne of Cleves, second and fourth wives of Henry VIII; Anne Frank, German–Jewish girl who kept a diary recording her family's persecution by the Nazis; Anna Freud, psychoanalyst; Anneka Rice and Anne Robinson, TV personalities; Annie Lennox, popular singer; Anna Ford, TV newscaster.

Annabel (f)
Variant of Anna, possibly a dissimilation of Amabel.
Variants Annabella, Anabel.

Anselm (m)
Italian, but of Germanic origin from the combined words for 'divinity', and 'helmet'. A rare name, used mainly by Roman Catholics in remembrance of Saint Anselm, the twelfth-century archbishop of Canterbury.
Variant Anselmo.

Anthea (f)
Greek, meaning 'flower, flowery'.
Variant Annthea.

Anthony (m)
From the Roman family name.
Variants Antony, Antoney, Antoine (French), Antonio (Italian/Spanish), Anton (German), Antonino.
Diminutive Tony (used independently).

Feminine Antonia, Antoinette, Antonina.
Diminutives Toni, Tonie, Tonia, Tonya.
Famous names Antony (Marcus Antonius), the Roman Triumvar renowned for his love affair with Cleopatra; Anthony Hopkins, actor; Anthony Burgess, novelist, author of *The Clockwork Orange.*

Antoinette (f)
French form of Anthony, popular in English-speaking countries.
Famous name Antoinette Sibley, ballerina.

Antonia (f)
Feminine form of Anthony, very popular in ancient Rome, and throughout Europe ever since.
Famous names Antonia Fraser, the writer of popular history, daughter of Lord Longford and married to the playwright, Harold Pinter; Antonia White, novelist.

Aphra (f)
Hebrew, meaning 'dust'.
Variant Afra.
Famous name Aphra Behn, acclaimed as being the first woman to make a living by writing.

April (f)
From the month.
Variants Avril, Avrile.

Arabella (f)
Latin, meaning 'yielding to prayer'.
Variant Arabelle.
Diminutive Bella.

Araminta (f)
Character in John Vanbrugh's comedy, *The Confederacy* (1705).

Variant Aminta.
Diminutives Minti, Minty.

Archibald (m)
Mainly a Scottish name, from the Germanic words for 'genuine' and 'brave'. Not popular in recent times.
Diminutive Archie.
Famous name Archie Gemmell, Scottish footballer.

Ariadne (f)
Greek, meaning 'holy one'.
Variant Ariane.

Arnold (m)
English and German name, made up of the words meaning 'eagle' and 'ruler'. There was an early saint bearing this name at the court of the Emperor Charlemagne, but it was rare from the Middle Ages until the nineteenth century.
Famous name Arnold Schwarzenegger, star of the *Terminator* movies.

Arthur (m)
Possibly Celtic, meaning 'bear'.
Feminine Artina, Artis, Arthuretta, Arthurina, Arthene, Artrice.
Famous names Arthur Ashe, the first black male to win a Grand Slam tournament. He became HIV+ after a heart operation and died of a related disease; Arthur Waley, poet and Chinese translator.

Ashley (m,f)
Old English, meaning 'ash wood'.
Variants Ashleigh, Ashlee, Ashlea.

Astrid (f)
Old Norse, meaning 'divine beauty'.
Variants Astri, Estrid.
Diminutives Asta, Assi, Atti.

Aubrey (m)
Norman, meaning 'elf power'.
Variants Aubary, Aubery, Aubury.

Audrey (f)
Old English, meaning 'noble strength'.
Variants Audra, Audree, Audreen.
Famous name Audrey Hepburn, Oscar-winning actress.

Augustus (m)
Latin, meaning 'great, venerable'.
Variants Augustin, Austin, Austen, Austyn, Ostin, Agustus.
Feminine Augusta, Augustina, Agusta.
Diminutives Gus, Gussie.
Famous names Augustus, the first Roman emperor; Augustus Hare, Victorian travel writer; Augustus John, painter.

Aurelia (f)
Latin family name meaning 'gold'.

Auriel (f)
Latin, meaning 'golden'.
Variants Auriol, Aureole.

Aurora (f)
Latin, the Roman goddess of dawn.
Variants Aurore, Aurea.

Austin (m)
An English contracted form of the Latin name Augustus, although its popular modern use may be a result of its frequent appearance as a surname.
Famous names Austin Clarke, Caribbean writer; Austin Mitchell, Member of Parliament.

Ava (f)
An English name of uncertain origin, although there was a ninth-century saint, Ava or Avia. Largely known because of the Hollywood actress Ava Gardner, who starred in films such as *Night of the Iguana* and was once voted the world's most beautiful woman.

Avril (f)
See April.

Axel (m)
From the Scandinavian name, Absalom.
Famous name Axel Munthe, author of bestselling *The Story of San Michele.*

B

Barbara (f)
Greek, meaning 'foreign woman'.
Variants Barbra, Babette (also variant of Elizabeth).
Diminutives Babs, Barbie.
Famous name Barbra Streisand, American singer and actress.

Barnabas (m)
Aramaic, meaning 'son of consolation'.
Variant Barnaby (more common than Barnabas).
Diminutive Barney.

Barry (m)
Irish, meaning 'spear'.
Famous names Barry Norman, television film critic and author; Barry McGuigan, boxer.

Bartholomew (m)
Aramaic, meaning 'son of Talmai'.
Variants Bartle, Bartlett.
Diminutives Bart, Barty, Bartie.

Basil (m)
Greek, meaning 'royal, kingly'.
Feminine Basille, Basilia, Basilie.
Famous name Cardinal Basil Hume.

Bathsheba (f)
Hebrew, meaning 'daughter of the oath'.
Diminutive Sheba (used independently).
Famous name Bathsheba is a character in Thomas Hardy's *Far from the Maddening Crowd* (1874).

Beatrice (f)
Latin, meaning 'bringer of joy, happiness'.
Variant Beatrix.
Diminutives Bea, Beatty, Trixie, Beattie.
Famous names Beatrice, the heroine of Shakespeare's *Much Ado About Nothing*; Beatrice Hastings, lover of Modigliani, the painter; Beatrix Potter, children's writer and illustrator.

Beau (m)
French, meaning 'handsome'.
Very popular in the Georgian and Victorian periods as a nickname for dandies such as Beau Brummell, and also often used to mean a young lady's admirer. It became a first name early in the twentieth century with its appearance in the novel *Beau Geste*, by P. C. Wren, and the character of Beau Wilks in Margaret Mitchell's *Gone with the Wind*.
Famous name Beau Bridges, American actor.

Belinda (f)
Possibly from the Italian word 'Bella' with -inda suffix, or from German, meaning 'dragon'.

Bella (f)
French, Italian, meaning 'beautiful'.
Variant Belle.

Benedict (m)
Latin, meaning 'blessed'.
Variants Bennet, Benet, Bengt, Benito.
Feminine Benedicta, Benita.
Diminutives Ben, Benny, Bennie.

Benjamin (m)
Hebrew, meaning 'son of my right hand'.
Variants Benejaman, Benjamen, Benjiman.
Diminutives Ben, Benny, Benjy, Benji.
Famous name Benjamin Disraeli, Victorian prime minister and novelist, favourite of Queen Victoria.

Berenice (f)
See Veronica.
Variant Bernice.
Famous name Berenice Abbott, photographer and pioneer of photography to illustrate the laws of physics.

Bernard (m)
Germanic, meaning 'bear strong'.
Variants Barnard, Bernhard.
Feminine Bernadette, Bernada, Bernadina.
Famous names St Bernadette of Lourdes had a series of visions of the Virgin Mary in her native village of Lourdes, now the largest place of pilgrimage in the Roman Catholic world; Bernadette Devlin, who became a Member of Parliament in her early twenties; Bernhard Langer, golfer.

Bertha, Berta (f)
Teutonic, meaning 'bright'.

Famous name Bertha, the mad wife of Rochester in Charlotte Bronte's novel, *Jane Eyre* (1847).

Bertram (m)
Old German, meaning 'bright raven'.
Variants Bertrand, Bartram.
Famous name Bertram Mills, circus owner; Bertrand Russell, philosopher.

Beryl (f)
English, taken from the pale green gemstone, a variety of emerald. Beryl, together with other gemstone names, became popular in late Victorian times.
Famous names Beryl Bainbridge, the novelist; Beryl Reid, actress and comedienne.

Beth (f)
Form of Elizabeth, became popular in America after the publication of Louisa M. Alcott's novel, *Little Women*, in which one of the four sisters is named Beth.

Betty (f)
From Elizabeth, used independently.
Variants Bette, Betsy, Bettina, Bettine, Betty Jo, Betty Lou.
Famous name Bette Davis, American film actress.

Beulah (f)
Hebrew, meaning 'married'.

Beverley (m,f)
Surname from the place name in Yorkshire, meaning 'beaver stream'.
Feminine Beverly.
Famous name Beverley Nichols, popular journalist and writer.

Bianca (f)
Italian, French, meaning 'white'.
Variants Blanch, Blanche, Candida.
Famous name Bianca Jagger, wife of the pop star.

Blair (m)
From Scottish surname, meaning 'flat land'.

Blake (m)
Surname from an Old English nickname, meaning either 'very dark' or 'very fair'.
Famous name Blake Edwards, film director.

Boaz (m)
Hebrew, meaning 'fleetness'.

Bob, Bobby
See Robert, Roberta.

Bonita (f)
Spanish, meaning 'pretty'.
Masculine Bonito.

Boyd (m)
Gaelic, meaning 'yellow'.

Bradley (m)
Old English, meaning 'broad clearing'.
Diminutive Brad.
Famous name Brad Pitt, popular American actor.

Brenda (f)
Old Norse, meaning 'sword'.

Brendan (m)
Irish, meaning 'stinking hair'.

Variants Brandon, Brendon
Famous names Brendan Foster, the athlete; Brendan Behan, Irish playwright.

Brett (m)
Latin, meaning 'Breton'.
Variant Bret.

Brian (m)
Origin uncertain, possibly Celtic, meaning 'hill' or 'noble'. Always a popular name, particularly in Ireland, where it is associated with one of the early kings of Ireland, Brian Boru.
Variant Bryan, Brien.
Feminine Briana, Brianna.
Famous names Brian Lara, West Indian cricketer; Brian Sewell, art critic.

Bridget (f)
Celtic, meaning 'the high one' or perhaps 'strength'.
Variants Bridgit, Brigid, Brigette, Brigitte, Brigitta.
Diminutives Bridge, Bridie, Biddie, Britt, Brita, Birgit.
Famous names St Bridget (Saint Bride), patroness of Ireland; actresses Britt Ekland and Brigitte Bardot; Bridget Brophy, novelist.

Bronwen (f)
Welsh, meaning 'fair/white breasted'.
Variant Bronwyn.

Bronya (f)
Russian name from Slavonic root, meaning 'armour' or 'protection'.

Brook (m,f)
From the surname.

Variant Brooke.
Famous name Brooke Shields, actress.

Bruce (m)
Scottish surname, possibly derived from Norman place name.
Famous names Robert 'the Bruce'; Bruce Willis, American actor; Bruce Forsyth, TV presenter.

Bruno (m)
Old German, meaning 'dark complexioned'.
Feminine Brunetta.

Bryce, Brice (m)
Celtic, origin uncertain.

Bryn (m)
Welsh, meaning 'hill'.

Bryony (f)
From the Greek word for a kind of moss, and also for a poisonous climber! One of many plant and flower names that became popular in the twentieth century.
Variant Briony.

Byron (m)
From the surname and Old English root word for 'cowshed'.

C

Caleb (m)
Hebrew, meaning 'dog' or 'bold'.

Calum, Callum (m)
Gaelic form of Columba, Scottish diminutive of Malcolm.

Calvin (m)
Latin, meaning 'bald'.
Variant Kalvin.
Famous name Calvin Klein, fashion designer.

Camelia (f)
From the flower name.
Variant Camellia.

Cameron (m)
From the Gaelic, meaning 'crooked nose'. Transferred surname from the great Highland clan of Cameron.

Camilla (f)
Old Roman family name, origin uncertain.
Variant Camille.

Diminutives Cammie, Millie, Milly.
Famous name Camilla Parker Bowles, friend of Prince Charles.

Campbell (m)
From the Gaelic meaning 'crooked mouth'. Like Cameron, this is a transferred surname from one of the major Highland clans, whose chief is the Duke of Argyll.

Candice (f)
Possibly derived from Latin, meaning 'white'.
Variant Candace.
Famous names Hereditary name of the Queens of Ethiopia until the fourth century; Candice Bergen, actress.

Candida (f)
Latin, meaning 'white'.
Variant See Bianca, Blanche, Candia, Candide.
Diminutives Candy, Candie.
Famous name Candia McWilliam, British novelist.

Cara (f)
Latin, meaning 'dear'.

Carl (m)
Variant Karl.
Feminine Carla, Carlene, Carly, Carley, Carlotta (see also Charlotte), Karla, Karlene, Karleen.
Famous names Carla Lane, television writer, wrote the popular television comedies: *The Liver Birds, Butterflies, Bread*; Carl Lewis, Olympic athlete; Charlotte Rampling, British actress.

Carmel (f)
Hebrew, meaning 'garden'.
English name of early Christian origin, referring to Our Lady of Carmel, one of the titles of the Virgin Mary. It is consequently a popular name with Roman Catholics.
Variants Carmela, Carmella, Carmilla, Carmelina (with diminutive Melina), Carmelita, Carmen.
Masculine Carmelo.

Carol (f)
Form of Charles, diminutive of Caroline.
Variants Carole, Carola, Carroll, Caroll, Caryl, Karel, Karol.
Masculine Carol, Carroll (Irish).
Famous name Carole King, American songwriter and singer.

Caroline (f)
Feminine form of Charles.
Variants Carolina, Carolin, Carolyn, Charlene, Carleen.
Diminutives Caro, Carol, Lina.
Famous name Caroline Charles, dress designer.

Cary (m)
Surname from the Celtic named River Cary in Somerset.
Famous name 'Cary Grant', London-born American actor born Archibald Leach.

Carys (f)
Welsh, meaning 'to love'.
Variants Cerys, Ceri, Cerri.

Caspar (m)
German form of Jasper.
Famous names One of the Three Wise Men (Caspar,

Balthasar and Melchior), who brought gifts to the newborn baby Jesus; Caspar Friedrich, German Romantic painter.

Cassandra (f)
Name from Greek legend – Cassandra was given the gift of second sight, but with the curse that no one would ever believe her prophecies. It has been popular since the Middle Ages in England and was the name of Jane Austen's favourite sister.
Diminutives Cass, Cassey, Cassie.

Catharine (f)
See Katharine for meaning.
Variants Catherine, Caterina, Catheryn, Cathleen, Caitlin, Catriona, Catrine, Caron, Caronne, Caryn.
Diminutives Cath, Cathy.
Famous names Name of several saints and Queens of England including three of the wives of Henry VIII.

Cecilia (f)
Roman clan name, possibly meaning 'blind'.
Variants Cecile, Cecily, Celia.
Masculine Cecil.
Famous names St Cecilia, patron saint of music; Cecil B. de Mille, legendary film director.

Celeste (f)
Latin, meaning 'heavenly'.
Variant Celestine.
Masculine Celestin with diminutive Celeste (French).

Celia (f)
English and Italian, from an old Roman family name probably meaning 'heaven'. Its popularity in this country has largely stemmed from its use in Shakespeare's comedy *As You Like It*.

Chantal (f)
French place name, meaning 'stone, boulder'.
Variants Chantalle, Chantel, Chantele, Shantel, Shantelle.

Charles (m)
Old English, meaning 'man, countryman'.
Popular throughout Europe and the English-speaking world, the name perhaps owes its original vogue to Charlemagne (literally 'Charles the Great'), the Frankish Emperor of the eighth century. It has been the name of many kings and princes.
Variants Siari (Welsh), Carl, Karl, Carlo, Carlos.
Diminutives Charlie, Charley, Chas, Chaz, Chuck.
Feminine Charleen, Charlaine, Carla, Carol, Caroline, Charlotte.
Famous names Prince Charles; Charles de Gaulle, French president and general; Charlie Chaplin, film actor, comedian, choreographer; Charles Baudelaire, French poet.

Charlotte (f)
Feminine of Charles.
Variants Carlotta, Charlotta.
Diminutives Lottie, Lotty, Totty, Charlie.
Famous name Charlotte Brontë, English novelist who wrote *Jane Eyre* (1847).

Charmaine (f)
From Roman clan name.
Variants Sharmain, Sharmaine, Sharmane.

Charmian (f)
Greek, meaning 'joy' (correct pronunciation 'Karmian').

Cher (f)
French, meaning 'dear'.

Variants Cherie, Sheri, Shereen, Sherena, Sherry, Cherilyn, Cheryl, Sherilyn.
Famous name Cher, American singer and actress.

Cherry (f)
English, probably the anglicized version of *chèrie*, or 'darling', but also nowadays taken as referring to the sweet fruit. It has a naughty meaning in the United States.

Cheryl (f)
A popular twentieth-century name, of unknown origin – possibly a crossing of Cherry and Beryl.

Chevonne (f)
See Siobahn.

Chloe (f)
Greek, meaning 'green shoot'.
Famous name Daphnis and Chloe, two characters in one of the classic Greek romances.

Christabel (f)
Combination of 'Christ' and 'Bella'.
Variants Christabella, Christobel, Chrystabel.
Famous name Christabel Pankhurst, British suffragette.

Christian (m)
Greek, meaning 'annointed'.
Variant Kristian.
Famous name Christian Lacroix, French fashion designer famous for his ostentatious creations.

Christine (f)
From Christiana, feminine form of Christian.
Variants Christina, Christiana, Cristen, Kristen, Kristian.

Diminutives Chris, Chrissie, Kirsty, Tina (used independently).
Famous names Christina Onassis, daughter of millionaire shipping magnate, Aristotle Onassis; Chrissie Hind, pop singer.

Christopher (m)
Greek, meaning 'one who bears Christ (within)'.
Variants Kristopher, Christof, Christoph.
Diminutives Chris, Kris, Kit.
Famous names St Christopher, patron saint of travellers; Christopher Colmbus, explorer; Chris Evert, American tennis champion who was the first woman tennis player to win $1 million in prize money; Christopher Isherwood, British novelist.

Chrystal (f)
Originally derived from Christopher.
Variants Crystal, Christal.
Diminutives Christie, Christy.
Famous name one of the lead female characters in the popular American soap, *Dynasty*.

Claire (f)
French, meaning 'clear, bright'.
Occasionally used as a male name.
Variants Clare, Clara, Clarissa, Clarice, Clarinda, Claribel.
Famous name In 1976, Clare Francis became the fastest yachtswoman to sail solo across the Atlantic.

Clarice (f)
English and French form of the Latin Claritia, meaning 'fame'. First used in medieval romance tales. The china ware of the 1920s Art Deco period, designed by Clarice Cliff, is now much sought after.

Variant Clarissa, famous for the eighteenth-century novel of the same name by Samuel Richardson.

Claud (m)
Latin, meaning 'lame'.
Variant Claude.
Feminine Claudia, Claudine, Claudette.
Famous name Claude Monet, French Impressionist painter, whose *Impression: Soleil levant* painting (1872), gave its name to the movement.

Clement (m)
Latin, meaning'merciful'.
Feminine Clementine, Clementina, Clemence, Clemency.
Diminutive Clem (m,f).
Famous name Clement Freud, cookery expert and Member of Parliament.

Clifford (m)
From surname and place name meaning 'cliff'.
Variants Cliff, Clifton, Clive.
Famous name Cliff Richard.

Clint (m)
Chiefly used in America, this is a transferred use of the surname, Clinton, which belonged to a great family of statesmen in the eighteenth and nineteenth centuries. Now famous largely because of the Hollywood actor, Clint Eastwood.
Variant Clinton.

Clive (m)
English, a transferred use of the surname, originating from a number of places and meaning 'cliff' or 'slope'.

Clover (f)
A modern flower name, used throughout the English-speaking world.

Colette(f)
Diminutive of Nicolette, see Nicola.
Variant Collette.
Famous name Sidonie Gabriel Colette, French novelist known by her surname.

Colin (m)
Diminutive of Nicholas, used independently.
Variant Colyn.
Feminine Colina, Colene, Coletta.
Famous names Colin Jackson, athlete; Colin Montgomery, golfer.

Colleen (f)
Irish, meaning 'girl'.
This has been a popular name in America and Australia ever since the fashion for Irish names during the 1940s, but is not often found as a Christian name in Ireland.

Conan (m)
Celtic, meaning 'wise'.

Conor (m)
Irish, meaning 'high desire'.
Variant Connor.

Conrad (m)
English and German, a variant spelling of Konrad, meaning 'bold counsel'. Its popularity in England dates from the nineteenth century.

Constant (m)
Latin, meaning 'constant, steadfast'.
Variant Constantine.
Feminine Contance, Constantia.
Famous name Constantine the Great, Roman Emperor after whom Constantinople (once Byzantium) was named.

Cora (f)
Greek, meaning 'maiden'.
Variants Coral, Coralie, Coralina, Coralena, Corinne.

Coral (f)
One of the group of names taken from semi-precious or precious stones, popularized during the late Victorian period. Coral is the beautiful pink gem that grows in warm seas and is often used to make jewellery.
Variant Coralie.

Cordelia (f)
English name of unknown origin, made famous by Shakespeare's use of it for his heroine, the king's youngest daughter, in *King Lear*.

Cornelia (f), **Cornelius** (m)
Latin, meaning 'horn'.

Cosmo (m)
From the Greek word, meaning 'order' or 'beauty'.
Popular in England, America, Italy and Germany. First brought to Britain by the dukes of Gordon, who had connections with Tuscany, in Italy.
Variant Cosimo, as in the famous Renaissance duke of Cosimo de' Medici.

Courtney (m,f)
From the aristocratic British surname.
Variants Courtenay, Courteney.

Craig (m)
Gaelic, meaning 'rugged rock'.

Cressida (f)
English, made famous first by Chaucer's and then Shakespeare's retelling of the legendary tale of Troilus and his faithless sweetheart Cressida. Thought to originate from the name of a Trojan girl captive, Chryseis, mentioned in Homer's *Iliad*, the name has become quite popular in the twentieth century.

Crispin (m)
Latin, meaning'curly haired'.
Variant Crispian.
Famous name St Crispin, patron saint of shoemakers who was martyred by being thrown ino molten lead.

Crystal (f)
English, one of a group of names adopted in the late nineteenth century from gems or semi-precious stones. Crystal is from the Greek word for 'ice'.
Variants Krystal, Krystle.

Curtis (m)
English surname, probably originating from the Old French, meaning 'courteous'.

Cynthia (f)
Greek, another name for Diana or Artemis, the goddess of the moon.

Cyril (m)
English, derived from the Greek for 'lord' and borne by a large number of saints, as well as the Greek evangelist who took Christianity to Eastern Europe and whose name was given to the alphabet used there, Cyrillic. Now declined in popularity.
Famous name Cyril Fletcher, comedian.

D

Daisy (f)
Anglo Saxon, flower name meaning 'eye of day'.
Famous name Daisy Ashford was just 11 years old when she wrote the book *The Young Visitors* in 1892.

Dale (m,f)
Anglo Saxon, meaning 'dweller in a valley'.

Daly, Daley (m)
From the Irish surname.

Damian, Damien (m)
Possibly derived from Damon, relates to one of two Greek brothers who were martyred in the early fourth century.

Damon (m)
From the Greek, meaning 'to subdue' or 'tame'. Famous from the Greek legend of Damon and Pythias, two friends who were each wiling to give up their lives for the other. Currently enjoying considerable popularity in Britain.

Famous names Damon Hill, racing driver; Damon Runyan, American short story writer.

Dane (m)
Old Norse, meaning native of Denmark.

Daniel (m)
Hebrew, meaning 'God is my judge'.
Diminutives Dan, Danny.
Feminine Danielle, Daniella, Danette, Daneen, Danita, Danna, Danya.
Diminutives Dana, Danni, Danny.
Famous name Daniel Deronda (1876) was the last of George Eliot's great novels

Dante (m)
Latin, meaning'enduring'.
Famous name Dante Alighieri, Italian poet.

Daphne (f)
Greek, meaning 'bay-tree, laurel'.

Darrell (m)
Transferred use of the surname originally belonging to a Norman family, the d'Airelles, from Airelle in Calvados, its first English use occurring in the late nineteenth century.
Variant Darryl.

Darren (m)
English of uncertain derivation, and of relatively recent appearance. Especially popular in America.

David (m)
Hebrew, meaning 'beloved, darling'. Name of the greatest of the Israelite kings, whose history is told in

the Book of Samuel. He slew the giant Philistine Goliath with his slingshot. Often a Jewish name in America, but has long been widespread in Britain, especially Wales, where it is the name of the patron saint.
Variants Dewi, Dafydd (Welsh).
Diminutives Dave, Davy, Dai, Taffy (Welsh).
Feminine Davida, Davina, Divina, Divinia, Vida, Vidette.
Famous names St David; David Bowie, singer/ musician; David Niven, British actor; David Hockney, artist; David Soul, TV actor in *Starsky and Hutch*; David Campese, rugby player.

Dawn (f)
From the Greek, meaning 'daybreak' (see Aurora, Aurore).
Famous names Dawn French, actress and comedienne; Dawn Fraser, Olympic swimmer.

Dean (m)
From the Old English surname.

Deanna (f)
See Diana.

Deborah (f)
Hebrew, meaning 'a bee'.
Variants Debora, Debra, Debrah, Devorah, Melissa (Greek equivalent of Deborah).
Diminutives Deb, Debbie, Debra.
Famous name Debbie Harry, singer with the pop group Blondie.

Declan (m)
Early Irish saint (Deaglan), linked with Ardmore.

Famous name Elvis Costello, singer songwriter who was born Declan Patrick McManus.

Deirdre (f)
Celtic, meaning 'raging one'.
In Irish legend Deirdrie was a tragic heroine, crossed in love, who eventually died of a broken heart.
Variants Deidra, Deirdrie.

Delia (f)
Greek, meaning 'from Delos'.
Famous name Delia Smith, cookery writer and television personality.

Delilah (f)
Hebrew, meaning 'delicate'.
Famous name Samson's mistress who betrayed him to the Philistines by cutting off his strength-giving hair.

Della (f)
English name, of unknown origin – perhaps a variant of Delia or Delilah – which appeared towards the end of the nineteenth century and has remained popular.

Delphine (f)
French and English, from the Latin term for a woman from Delphi. Now associated with the flower, delphinium.

Demelza (f)
Cornish name which became particularly popular in Britain during the 1950s, when a heroine of that name appeared in the television adaptation of the 'Poldark' novels, by Winston Graham.

Denis (m)
Greek, from Dionysius, god of wine.
Variants Dennis, Denys.
Feminine Denise, Denyse, Deniece, Denize.
Diminutives Den, Denny.
Famous names St Denis, patron saint of Paris, beheaded in 272; Denis Healey, English politician who was Chancellor of the Exchequer in the 1970s; Dennis Potter, TV playwright; Dennis the Menace, cartoon character in the *Beano*; Denise Robbins, romantic novelist.

Denzel (m)
Cornish place name and sixteenth-century family name.
Variants Denzil, Denzill, Denzyl.
Diminutives Derrie, Derry (used independently for girls and boys).
Famous name Denzil Washington, American actor.

Derek (m)
Low German, from Theodoric meaning 'people's ruler'. Though common in Britain, rarely found in the USA.
Variants Derick, Derrick, Deric, Dirk (Dutch).
Diminutives Derrie, Derry.
Famous name Derek Jacobi, English Shakespearean actor.

Dermot (m)
Celtic, meaning 'free from envy'.
Variant Diarmid.

Derry (f)
English of unknown origin.

Dervla (f)
Irish, from the Gaelic Deirbhile, meaning 'daughter poet'.

Variant Dervila.
Famous name Dervla Murphy, twentieth-century travel writer.

Desdemona (f)
English name from heroine of Shakespeare's *Othello*, probably derived from the Greek word meaning 'ill-fated'.

Desiree (f)
French, meaning, 'desired'.
Masculine Didier (French).

Desmond (m)
Celtic clan name, from Munster in Ireland.
Diminutives Des, Desy.

Dewi (m)
Welsh version of David, which has become very popular.
Famous name Saint Dewi flourished in the fifth century.

Dexter (m)
Latin, meaning'right handed'.

Diana (f)
Latin, meaning 'bright one'. In Roman mythology, Diana was goddess of the moon, chastity and hunting.
Variants Dian, Diane, Dianna, Dyana, Dyan, Deanna, Deanne.
Diminutive Di.
Famous names Diane de Poitiers, favourite of French King Henri II; Dame Diana Rigg, actress known for her role as Emma Peel in *The Avengers*; Diana Ross, popular singer.

Dick (m)
See Richard.

Dickie (m)
See Richard.

Didier (m)
French, meaning 'longing'. Popular name in France.

Dieter (m)
Old German, meaning 'race' and 'warrior'.

Dillon (m)
See Dylan.

Dilly (f)
See Dilys and Dilwen.

Dilwen (f)
Modern Welsh name combining Dilys and Gwyn, meaning 'fair, holy'.
Diminutive Dilly.

Dilys (f)
Welsh, meaning 'perfect'.
Diminutive Dilly.
Famous name Dilys Powell, film and theatre critic.

Dina (f)
See Dinah.

Dinah (f)
Biblical, meaning 'judgement'. Dinah appears in the Book of Genesis. Also a variant of Diana.
Variant Dina.

Dion (m)
Diminutive of Dionysos, the Greek god of wine.
Feminine Dionne, Dione.

Dirk (m)
Flemish and Dutch version of Derek.
Famous name Dirk Bogarde, film actor and writer.

Dodie (f)
See Dorothy.

Dolly (f)
See Dorothy.

Dolores (f)
Spanish, meaning 'sorrows'.
Diminutives Lola, Lolita (used independently).
Famous name Vladimir Nabokov's novel of a precocious teenage girl *Lolita*.

Dominic (m)
Latin, meaning 'born on the Lord's day'. Originally given to children born on Sunday.
Feminine Dominica, Dominique.
Famous name Saint Dominic, twelfth-century founder of the Dominican order of monks.

Dominica (f)
See Dominic.

Don (m)
See Donald.

Donagh (m)
Irish, from the Gaelic Donnchadh, see also Duncan.

Donal (m)
See Donald.

Donald (m)
Gaelic, meaning, 'ruler of the world'.
Variants Donal, Donagh, Donaidh.
Diminutives Don, Donny.
Feminine Donaldina, Donalda, Donella, Donita.
Famous names Donald Sutherland, American actor; Donny Osmond, popular '70s singer.

Donna (f)
Italian, meaning 'lady of the house'.
English and Scottish twentieth-century name.
Either a female version of Don, or a contraction of Madonna.

Donovan (m)
Irish surname, meaning 'dark brown'.
Variant Donavon.
Famous name Donovan Leitch, known professionally by his first name only. Hailed as the British answer to Bob Dylan.

Dora (f)
See Dorothy, Isidora, Theodora.

Dorcas (f)
From Greek, meaning 'doe'. Common Puritan name in sixteenth century and still in use today.

Dorean (f)
From Gaelic, meaning daughter of Finn. A popular twentieth-century name.

Doreen (f)
English diminutive of Dora.
Variants Dorene, Dorine.

Dorian (m)
Greek, meaning 'man from Doris'.
Feminine Doria, Doris, Dorinda, Dorita.
Famous name The main character in Oscar Wilde's novel *The Picture of Dorian Gray* (1891).

Doris (f)
English and German, derived from a tribal name in ancient Greece and the Greek goddess of the sea. Very popular pre-1930s.
Famous names Doris Day, film actress; Doris Lessing, South African writer.

Dorothea (f)
Greek, meaning 'a gift from God'. Popular in nineteenth century but now rarely used, having given way to Dorothy – see below.
Variant Thea.
Famous names Saint Dorothea, a third-century martyr, always presented surrounded by roses and fruit; Dorothea Brooke, heroine of George Eliot's *Middlemarch* (1872).

Dorothy (f)
English version of Dorothea.
Variants Dorothée, Doreen, Dora.
Diminutives Dolly, Dot, Dottie, Dodie.
Famous names Dorothy Wordsworth, sister of the Romanic poet; Dorothy L. Sayers, English detective novelist; Dolly Parton, American Country and Western singer; Dora Carrington, English painter.

Dot (f)
See Dorothy.

Dottie (f)
See Dorothy.

Dougal (m)
Scottish, from Gaelic Dughall, meaning 'dark stranger'.
Variants Dugald, Dugal.
Diminutive Dougie.

Douglas (m)
Gaelic, meaning 'dark stream', a Scottish clan name of the earls of Douglas and Angus.
Diminutives Doug, Duggie.
Famous name 'Black Douglas', thirteenth-century champion of Robert Bruce and dreaded by the English.

Drew (m)
See Andrew.

Drusilla (f)
From the Latin, meaning 'strengthening'.
Famous names Caligula's sister and mistress. Also a Jewish woman converted to Christianity by Saint Paul (see Acts XXIV).

Duald (m)
From Gaelic Dubhaltach, meaning 'black-haired'.

Duane (m)
From the Gaelic, meaning 'dark'.
Variants Dwain, Dwaine, Dwane, Dwayne.
Famous name Duane Eddy, pop singer and guitarist.

Dudley (m)
Originally a surname from the West Midlands derived from Old English, meaning 'wood or clearing of Dudda'.

Famous names Robert Dudley, the Earl of Leicester who was much liked by Queen Elizabeth I; Dudley Moore, actor and comedian.

Duff (m)
Scottish, probably meaning 'dark'.

Duggie (m)
See Douglas.

Duke (m)
English, a shortened form of Marmaduke which exists in its own right.
Famous names Duke Ellington, jazz pianist and composer; Duke Hussey, director general of the BBC.

Dulcie (f)
From Latin, meaning 'sweet'.
Famous name Dulcie Gray, actress.

Duncan (m)
Gaelic, meaning 'brown warrior'.
Famous names Saints Duncan, seventh-century Scottish saint, abbot of Iona, and tenth-century Irish saint, abbot of Clonmacnois; King of Scotland murdered by Macbeth in Shakespeare's play; Duncan Goodhew, British Olympic swimmer.

Dunstan (m)
Anglo Saxon, meaning 'hill-stone'.

Dustin (m)
Possibly from Old Norse, meaning 'Thor's stone'. Became popular in late twentieth century.
Feminine Dusty.
Famous names Dustin Hoffman, American film actor; Dusty Springfield, pop singer.

Dwane (m)
See Duane.

Dylan (m)
Welsh, meaning 'the sea'.
Famous name Dylan Thomas, Welsh poet famous for *Under Milk Wood* (1954).

Dymphna (f)
From Gaelic, meaning 'fawn'.
Variant Dympna.
Famous names Saint Dymphna, daughter of a sixth-century Irish chieftain and patron saint of the insane; Dymphna Cusack, Irish actress.

E

Eamonn (m)
Irish form of Edmund.
Variant Eamon.
Famous names Eamon de Valera, president of Ireland; Eamonn Andrews, TV presenter.

Earl (m)
Old English, meaning 'a noble'.

Ed (m)
See Edward.

Eddie (m)
See Edward.

Eden (m,f)
Hebrew, meaning 'delight'.

Edgar (m)
Anglo-Saxon, meaning 'fortunate spear'.
Variant Edgard.
Famous names Edgar Allan Poe, American mystery and

detective writer; Edgar Wallace, American crime writer; Edgar Lustgarten, British crime writer.

Edith (f)
Old English name, meaning 'riches' and 'strife'.
Variants Edythe, Edyta.
Diminutive Edie.
Famous name Edith Wharton, American novelist; Edith Piaf, popular French singer.

Edmond, Edmund (m)
Anglo-Saxon, meaning 'prosperity' and 'protection'.
Famous name Sir Edmund Hillary, New Zealand mountain climber and explorer.

Edna (f)
Hebrew, meaning 'pleasure, happiness'.
Popular first in Ireland.
Famous names Edna St Vincent Millay, poet; Edna O'Brien, Irish novelist.

Edward (m)
Anglo-Saxon, meaning 'guardian of prosperity'.
A name that remains constantly popular.
Variants Eideard, Edouard, Eduardo, Duarte, Edward.
Diminutives Ed, Eddie, Ned, Neddy, Ted, Teddy.
Famous names Eight English kings, the last being Edward VIII (1936) who voluntarily abdicated in order to marry a divorcee, Wallis Simpson; Edward Lear, celebrated for his nonsense rhymes, such as 'The Owl and the Pussycat', his paintings and travel writings; Edward Elgar, English composer; Eddy Murphy, American film actor; Eduardo Paolozzi, Scottish pop artist; Edward Blishen, children's book illustrator.

Edwin (m)
Old English, meaning 'rich friend'.
Feminine Edwina, Edweena, Edwyna.
Famous names Edwina Currie, Conservative politician and author.

Effie (f)
Diminutive form of Euphemia, meaning 'good speaking', now used in its own right.

Egon (m)
German medieval name meaning 'sword point'.
Famous name Egon Ronay, author of the *Good Food Guide.*

Eileen (f)
Irish, originally from the Gaelic *Eibhlin* which itself is derived from Evelyn or Helen.
Variants Aileen, Ayleen, Eilean, Ilene.
Diminutives Eily, Eiley.

Eirian (f)
Welsh, meaning 'silver'.
Variants Arian, Ariane.

Eireen (f)
See Irene.

Elaine (f)
See Helen.

Eleanor (f)
Possibly a derivation of Helen, the name was introduced by Eleanor of Aquitaine, the wife of Henry II.
Variants Eleanora, Eleanore, Elinor.
Diminutives Lenore, Lenora, Leonora, Ella, Nora, Nellie, Ellie.
Famous name Eleanor Bron, English actress.

Elfreda (f)
Victorian revival of Anglo-Saxon name, meaning 'elf strength'.
Variants Alfreda, Elfrieda, Elfriede, Elfrida.
Diminutives Elfi, Freda.

Eli (m)
Hebrew, meaning 'exalted'.

Eliot, Elliott (m)
Scottish surname, originally derived from Eli.

Elise (f)
See Elizabeth.

Eliza (f)
See Elizabeth.

Elizabeth (f)
Hebrew, meaning 'oath of God'.
Variants Elisabeth, Lisbeth, Liza, Lisa, Lisette, Elspeth, Bettina, Betsy, Elisa, Elise, Eliza, Lilly, Elsa, Elsie.
Diminutives Beth, Bess, Bessy, Betty, Liz, Lizzy, Libby.
Famous names Queen Elizabeth I first popularized the name in the fifteenth century; Elizabeth Barrett Browning, English writer and poet; Liz Hurley, film actress; Elizabeth Bowe, novelist; Elizabeth Frink, sculptress; Elizabeth Fritsch, potter.

Elke (f)
Dutch name, short for Adelheid, and Jewish female variation of Elkan.
Diminutive Elkie.
Famous names Elke Sommers, film actress; Elkie Brooks, singer.

Ella (f)
Possibly shortened form of Eleanor or Elvira, current since the eleventh century.
Famous name Ella Fitzgerald, jazz singer.

Ellen (f)
Originated from Helen, now an entirely separate name.

Ellie (f)
See Eleanor.

Elmer (m)
English and American, meaning 'noble and famous'.
Famous name Elmer Gantry, film starring Burt Lancaster.

Eloïse (f)
See Heloïse and Louise.

Elroy (m)
Variant of Leroy, meaning 'the king'.

Elsa (f)
English, German and Swedish.
Famous name Elsa, the Lioness, star of Joy Adamson's book and the film *Born Free*.

Elsie (f)
English and Scottish name, diminutive of Alice, Elizabeth or Elspeth, used in its own right and very popular at the beginning of this century.

Elspeth (f)
Scottish variant of Elizabeth.
Famous name Elspeth Huxley, writer.

Elton (m)
Derived from surname based on English place names.
Famous name Elton John, popular singer, songwriter.

Elvira (f)
Of Spanish and German origins, popular in medieval times and still popular in the twentieth century, meaning 'other truth'.
Famous name Don Juan's wife in Lord Byron's epic poem.

Elvis (m)
American, of unknown origin and meaning.
Famous name Elvis Presley, rock 'n' roll singer, from whom its current popularity derives.

Emanuel (m) **Emanuelle** (f)
Hebrew, meaning 'God is with us'.
Variants Manuel (m), Manuela (f)

Emeline (f)
Teutonic, origin uncertain.
Variants Emmeline, Emiline, Emmalene, Emlyn (not the same as Welsh Emlyn).

Emerald (f)
Spanish, meaning 'emerald'.
Variant Esmeralda.

Emil, Emile (m)
Latin, meaning 'eager'.
Feminine Emily.
Famous names Emily Brontë, author of *Wuthering Heights*; Emily Dickinson, American poet, known for her hermetic writing; Emil Nolde, German Expressionist painter.

Emlyn (m)
Welsh, meaning 'work serpent'.
Famous name Emlyn Williams, Welsh actor.

Emma (f)
Teutonic, meaning 'entire, all'.
Famous name Title and main character in a novel by much-loved English author, Jane Austen.

Emrys (m)
Welsh variant of Ambrose.

Ena (f)
Anglicized variant of Gaelic Eithne.
Famous name Ena Sharples, a character in British soap, *Coronation Street.*

Engelbert (m)
Old German, meaning 'bright Angle'.
Variant Englebert.
Famous names Saint Engelbert, thirteenth-century bishop of Cologne; Englebert Humperdinck, pop musician.

Enid (f)
Celtic, meaning 'spotless purity'.
Famous name Enid Blyton, children's writer.

Enoch (m)
Biblical name, from the Hebrew, meaning 'dedicated'.
Famous name Enoch Powell, British politician and classical scholar.

Ephraim (m)
Hebrew, meaning 'fruitful'.

Erin (f)
Irish, from Gaelic Eirinn, meaning 'for Ireland'. Currently very popular in Ireland and USA.

Eric (m)
Norse, meaning 'forever king'.
Variant Erik.
Feminine Erica, Erika.
Famous names Erica Jong, writer and poet, best known for her novel *Fear of Flying*; Eric Morecambe, comedian.

Erland (m)
Old Norse, meaning 'foreigner'.

Ernest (m)
Teutonic, meaning 'serious'.
Feminine Ernestine, Ernestina.
Variant Ernst.
Diminutives Ern, Ernie.
Famous names Ernest Hemingway, American novelist and short story writer, author of *For Whom the Bell Tolls*; Ernie Wise, comedian of the Morecambe and Wise partnership.

Errol (m)
Derived fom Scottish surname, in turn derived from place name.
Variant Erroll.
Famous names Errol Flynn, film actor; Erroll Garner, jazz pianist.

Erskine (m)
Scottish and Irish, based on a place name.
Famous name Erskine Childers, political activist and author of *The Riddle of the Sands*.

Esma (f), **Esme** (m,f)
French, meaning, 'esteemed'.

Esmond (m)
Teutonic, meaning 'divine protector'.
Variant Esmund.

Estella (f)
Latin, meaning 'star'.
Variants Estelle, Stella.

Esther (f)
Persian, from name of Persian goddess Ishtar. In the Bible the name of a Jewish woman who married the Persian King Ahasuerus.
Variants Hester, Ester.
Famous name Esther Rantzen, television star.

Ethan (f)
Hebrew name meaning 'long-lived'.
Variant Eitan
Famous name Ethan Frome, a novel of passion and vengeance by Edith Wharton.

Ethel (f)
Germanic, meaning 'noble', shortened form of Ethelburga and Etheldreda, and now used in its own right, particularly at the beginning of the twentieth century.

Etta (f)
English and Scottish short variant of names ending with that suffix, now used in is own right. In Italian, the suffix 'etta' means 'little'.

Eudora (f)
Greek, meaning 'good gift'.

Eugene (m)
Greek, meaning 'well-born'.
Diminutive Gene.
Feminine Eugenie, Eugenia.
Diminutive Gena.
Famous name Eugene O'Neill, American playwright.

Eunice (f)
Greek, meaning 'victorious'.
Famous name Eunice, the biblical mother of Timothy whom she introduced to Christianity.

Euphemia (f)
Greek, meaning 'well spoken of'.

Eustace (m)
Greek, meaning 'good harvest'.

Eva (f)
Hebrew, meaning 'life'.
Variant Eve.
Famous names Eva Peron, commonly known as 'Evita', wife of former President of Argentina, Juan Perón.

Evan (m)
Welsh form of John.
Famous name Evan Hunter, American novelist, author of *The Blackboard Jungle.*

Evangeline (f)
Greek, meaning 'good news'.

Evelyn (m,f)
From Norman French, of uncertain meaning.
Variants Eveline, Evelyne.
Famous name Evelyn Waugh, satirical novelist

Ewan (m)
Uncertain origin, possibly meaning 'youth'.
Variants Ewen, Euan

Ezra (m)
Hebrew, meaning 'help'.
Famous name Ezra Pound, American poet.

F

Fabian (m)
Latin, meaning 'bean grower'.
Variant Fabius.
Feminine Fabia, Fabiana.

Faith (f)
Latin, one of the virtues.
Variants Fay, Faye.

Fanny (f)
Diminutive of Frances, but used in its own right, particularly in the nineteenth century. Used less now because of naughty connotations.
Famous names Fanny Trollope, Anthony Trollope's adventurous writer mother; Fanny Burney, prodigious and lively novelist and lady-in-waiting to Queen Charlotte.

Farquhar (m)
Gaelic, meaning 'dear one'.

Farrer (m), **Farrah** (f)
Latin, meaning 'iron'.

Faustina (f)
Latin, meaning 'fortunate, lucky'.
Variants Fortuna, Lucky.

Fay (f)
Old English name, meaning 'fairy'.
Variants Faye, Fae.
Famous names Fay Dunaway, American actress; Fay Weldon, witty author of *The Life and Loves of a She-Devil* and other novels.

Felicity (f)
From Latin, meaning 'happy'.
Masculine Felix, which is becoming a popular name.
Diminutives Flic, Flick, Lissy.
Famous names Felicity Kendal, English actress.

Felix (m)
Latin, meaning 'happy'.
Feminine Felicia, Felicity.

Fenella (f)
Gaelic, meaning 'fair shoulders'.
Variants Fionola, Finola, Fionnuala.
Famous name Fenella Fielding, witty English actress.

Fenton (m)
Old English, meaning 'town on the marsh'.

Ferdinand (m)
Teutonic, meaning 'adventurous'.

Fergal (m)
Irish from Gaelic Fearghal, meaning 'man of valour'.

Fergus (m)
Celtic, meaning 'chosen man'.
Variant Feargus.
Diminutive Fergie.

Fernley (m)
Cornish, origin unknown, but popular in that area.

Fidel (m) **Fidelia** (f)
Latin, meaning'faithful'.
Famous name Fidel Castro, Cuban revolutionary and subsequent President of Cuba.

Fingal (m)
Celtic, meaning 'pale stranger'.

Finlay (m)
Gaelic, meaning 'fair hero'.

Fiona (f)
Scottish, from Gaelic, meaning 'fair, white'.
Famous name Fiona Pitt-Kethley, risqué poet.

Fitz, Fitzroy (m)
Norman, meaning 'son'.

Flavia (f) **Flavian** (m)
Latin, meaning 'golden haired'.

Fleur (f)
French, meaning 'flower'.
Variants Flora, Florinda, Fleurette, Florrie.
Masculine Florian.
Fames name Fleur, daughter of Soames Forsyte in John Galsworthy's popular *Forsyte Saga*.

Florence (f)
Latin, meaning 'blooming'.
Diminutives Flo, Florrie, Flossie.
Famous name Florence Nightingale, famous English nurse.

Fran (f)
See Frances.

Frances (f)
Latin, meaning 'French person, a Frank'.
Variants Francesca, Francine, Franceen, Francene, Francisca, Francoise.
Diminutives Franny, Fran, Francie, Frankie.
Masculine Francis, Francisco, Franco, Franz, Frank.
Famous names Françoise Sagan, won the *Prix des Critiques* for her first novel, *Bonjour Tristesse*, written when she was eighteen; Saint Francis of Assisi; Francis Bacon, Elizabethan philosopher; Francis Bacon, controversial twentieth-century painter; Francis King, novelist; Frank Bruno, boxer.

Frank (m)
See Frances.

Fraser (m)
From the surname, based on a French place name.
Variant Frazer.

Freda (f)
Diminutive of Elfrida, Frederica or Winifred; used independently.
Variants Frida, Frieda.

Frederick (m)
German, meaning comprised of 'peace' and 'power'.
Variants Frederic, Fredric.
Feminine Freda, Frederica, Frederique, Frida, Frieda.
Diminutives Fred (m,f), Freddie.
Famous names Frederick I, II, III, rulers of the Holy Roman Empire; Fred Perry, tennis champion.

Freya (f)
Old Norse, goddess of love, a traditional name of the Shetlands and Scotland.
Famous name Freya Stark, intrepid travel writer.

G

Gabriel (m)
Hebrew, meaning 'man of God'. In the Bible, Gabriel is one of the archangels, God's chief messenger, sometimes the Angel of Death, sometimes Prince of Fire and Thunder.
Variants Gabriele, Gabor.
Feminine Gabriella, Gabrielle.
Diminutives Gaby, Gabi.

Gaia (f)
From Greek Gaea, goddess of the earth.

Gail (f)
Short form of Abigail, came into independent usage in the middle of the twentieth century.
Variants Gael, Gaile, Gaila, Gale, Gayle.
Famous name Gayle Hunnicutt, American film actress.

Gareth (m)
Welsh, meaning 'gentle'.
Diminutives Gary (used independently).

Garrett (m)
Irish form of Gerald and Gerrard.
Variant Garrett.
Famous name Garret FitzGerald, former prime minister of Ireland.

Garry (m)
See Gary.

Garth (m)
See Gareth.

Gary (m)
English, from surname meaning 'spear'.
Diminutive Gaz.
Famous names Gary Cooper, American film actor; Gary Glitter, pop star; Gary Sobers, cricketer; Gary Lineker, soccer player.

Gavin (m)
Celtic, meaning 'white hawk'.
Variant Gawain.
Famous names Sir Gawain from Arthurian legend, nephew of King Arthur; Gavin Ewart, witty poet and master of the limerick; Gavin Hastings, rugby player.

Gaynor (f)
From Welsh, meaning 'beautiful maiden', a medieval variation of Guinevere of Arthurian legend.
Variant Gaenor.

Gay (f)
Once upon a time this meant 'cheerful' and was a popular name. Now little used because of its recent connotation of homosexuality.
Variants Gaye, Gae.

Gemma (f)
Italian, meaning 'gem, precious stone'.
Variant Jemma.

Gene (m)
Diminutive of Eugene, now popular in its own right, particularly in the United States.
Famous names Gene Pitney, popular singer; Gene Hackman, American film actor.

Genevieve (f)
Origin uncertain, perhaps meaning 'people' or 'woman'.
Diminutives Ginette, Ginetta.
Famous name St Genevieve, patron saint of Paris.

Geoff (m)
See Geoffrey.

Geoffrey (m)
Origin uncertain, possibly a variant of Godfrey.
Variant Jeffrey.
Diminutives Geoff, Jeff.
Famous names Jeffrey Archer, popular novelist; Jeff Bridges, American actor.

George (m)
Greek, meaning 'farmer'.
Feminine Georgeana, Georgia, Georgina, Georgiana, Georgette, Georgine.
Diminutives Georgie, Gina.
Famous names Six English kings; George Gershwin, American composer; George Eliot, author of *Middlemarch* and *The Mill on the Floss*; George Sand, writer and lover of Chopin; George Best, footballer; George Grosz, German satirical artist; George Michael, pop singer.

Georgie (m,f)
See George.

Geraint (m)
Welsh. Geraint was one of the knights of King Arthur's Round Table. Now very popular in Wales.
Famous name Geraint Evans, Welsh opera singer.

Gerald (m), **Geraldine** (f)
Norman, comprised of 'spear' and 'ruler'.
Diminutives Gerry, Jerry.
Famous names Gerald du Maurier, author of *Trilby*.

Gerard (m)
Norman, comprised of 'spear' and 'brave'.
Variants Gerrard, Jerrard, Gerhard, Gerrit, Garrit.
Famous name Gerard de Nerval, French Romantic writer.

Gerda (f)
Scandinavian, based on the name of the god Frey's wife.
Variant Gerde.

Germaine (f)
English and French, female version of Germain, meaning 'brother'.
Famous name Germaine Greer, Australian feminist.

Gerry (m,f)
Diminutive of Gerald, or Geraldine; sometimes used as a female name in its own right.

Gertrude (f)
Old German, comprised of 'spear' and 'beloved'.
Diminutives Gert, Gertie, Trudy, Trudi.
Famous names Gertrude Stein, American novelist.

Gervaise (m)
Norman, of Germanic origin, meaning 'spear-servant'. Usage is largely based on a fourth-century saint, Gervasius.
Variants Gervase, Jarvis, Gervasi.

Ghislain (f)
English based on Old French.
Variant Ghislaine.

Gilbert (m)
Norman, from German origin, comprised of 'pledge' and 'bright'.
Feminine Gilberta.
Famous name Gilbert White, author of *The Natural History of Selborne.*

Giles (m)
Greek, meaning 'young goat'. A humorous generic name for a farmer.
Famous names Saint Giles, patron saint of cripples; Giles Brandreth, journalist.

Gill (f)
See Gillian.

Gillian (f)
English form of Juliana.
Variants Jillian, Gilian, Gillianne, Jillianne.
Diminutives Gill, Jill, Jilly.
Masculine Gillean.
Famous names Jilly Cooper, author of *Polo* and other popular novels.

Gina (f)
Italian and English, diminutive of Georgina, now used in its own right.
Famous name Gina Lollobrigida, Italian film actress.

Ginny (f)
See Virginia.

Giovanna (f)
Feminine of Latin, Giovanni (John).

Giselle (f)
Old German, meaning 'pledge'.
Famous name *Giselle*, ballet, with music by Adolphe Adam.

Gladys (f)
Welsh version of Claudia.

Glanville (m)
Surname from Norman place name.
Variants Glenvil, Glenville.

Glen (m)
From the surname meaning 'valley dweller'.
Feminine Glenna, Glenn (also male).
Famous names Glenn Miller, American bandleader; Glenn Close, American actress.

Glenda (f)
Welsh, meaning 'pure and good'.
Famous name Glenda Jackson, actress and MP.

Glenys (f)
Modern Welsh, meaning 'pure and good'.
Variant Glynis.
Famous name Glenys Kinnock, Euro MP.

Gloria (f)
Latin, meaning 'glory'.
Variants Gloriana, Glory.
In Edmund Spenser's *Faerie Queene*, Gloriana was the allegorical name for Queen Elizabeth 1st.

Glyn (m)
Welsh, meaning 'valley'.
Variant Glynn.
Famous name Glyn Daniels, archaeologist.

Godfrey (m)
Norman, of Germanic origin, meaning 'good peace'.

Gordon (m)
Scottish clan name, uncertain origin.

Goronwy (m)
Welsh, of uncertain origin. Goronwy the Staunch appears in *The Mabinogion*.

Grace (f)
Latin, meaning 'grace'.
Diminutive Gracie.
Famous names Grace Jones, actress, model and singer; Grace Kelly, actress who became the wife of Prince Rainier of Monaco; Gracie Fields, popular singer.

Graeme (m)
English place name, Scottish clan name.
Variants Graham, Grahame.
Famous names Graham Gooch, English cricketer; Graeme Souness, soccer player.

Grania (f)
Irish, meaning 'loved'.
Variants Grainne, Grainnia.

Grant (m)
From the surname meaning 'large'.

Greg (m)
See Gregory.

Gregory (m)
Greek, meaning 'watchful'. An early Christian name.
Variants Gregor (Scottish), Gregoire, Gregg.
Diminutive Greg.
Famous names Saint Gregory, a sixth-century Pope who gave his name to Gregorian chant. His feast day is on 12 March; Gregory Peck, American film actor.

Gresham (m)
From the surname and place name.

Griselda (f)
Uncertain origin, possibly comprised of 'grey' and 'battle'.
Variant Zelda.
Famous names Zelda Sayre married Scott Fitzgerald after the publication of his first novel, *This Side of Paradise* (1920).

Greta (f)
See Margaret.
Variant Gretchen.
Famous name Greta Garbo, Swedish film actress.

Guinevere (f)
Welsh via Old French, meaning 'fair and smooth'.
She was the beautiful wife of King Arthur who fell in love with Sir Lancelot.

Gus (m)
See Augustus, Augustine.

Guy (m)
From the German root, meaning 'wood' or 'wide'.
Famous names Guy Fawkes; Guy de Maupassant, French author.

Gwendolen (f)
Welsh, meaning 'white-browed'.
Variants Gwendolin, Gwendolyn, Gwendoline.
Diminutives Gwen, Gwennie.
Famous name Gwen Watkins, actress.

Gwyneth (f)
Welsh, feminine variant of Gwynedd.

H

Hadrian (m)
See Adrian.

Hal (m)
Diminutive of Harry/Henry.

Halcyon (f)
Greek, meaning 'mythical bird'.

Haley (m)
See Hayley.

Hamilton (m)
From the surnme and place name.

Hamish (m)
Gaelic for James.
Famous name Hamish MacInnes, mountaineer.

Hank (m)
English medieval, now American diminutive of Henry.

Hannah (f)
Hebrew, meaning 'God has favoured me'.
Famous names Biblical mother of the prophet Samuel; Hannah Gordon, English actress.

Harold (m)
Old English, meaning 'army ruler'.
Feminine Haralda, Haroldene.
Famous names Harold Fairhair (Harold I), King of Norway; Harold Wilson and Harold Macmillan, prime ministers of Britain.

Harris (m)
From the surname.
Variant Harrison.
Famous name Harrison Ford, American actor.

Harry (m)
Diminutive of Henry, used independently.
Feminine Harriet, Harriot, Harriott.
Diminutives Hattie, Hatty.
Famous names 'Dirty Harry', a film character played by Clint Eastwood; Harriet Martineu, nineteenth-century writer and social reformer; Harry S. Truman, US president.

Hartley (m)
English, derived from surname, which in turn is derived from a place name, meaning 'deer and wood'.
Famous name Hartley Coleridge, eldest son of Samuel Taylor Coleridge.

Harvey (m)
Celtic, meaning 'battleworthy'.
Famous names Harvey Smith, showjumper; Harvey Keitel, film actor.

Hattie (f)
See Harriet.

Hayden (m)
From the surname and place name.
Variant Hadyn.

Hayley (f)
Derived from English place name.
Variant Haley.
Famous name Hayley Mills, English actress.

Hazel (f)
English, from the nutbush, and brown/green eye colour. Popular since the nineteenth century.

Heath (m)
From the surname.
Famous name Heath Robinson, English artist, cartoonist and book illustrator.

Heather (f)
English, from the moorland purple and mauve flowering plants.
Famous name Heather Cooper, astronomer.

Hebe (f)
Greek, meaning 'youth' and the goddess of youth.

Heidi (f)
Swiss variant of Adelaide.
Famous name The heroine of the children's novel *Heidi* by Johanna Spyri.

Helen (f)
Greek, meaning 'shining'.

Variants Helena, Helene, Halina, Ellen, Elaine.
Famous names Helen of Troy; Helena Rubenstein, cosmetics empire founder; Elaine Page, singer.

Helga (f)
Scandinavian, from Old Norse meaning 'happy'.
Variants Hella, Helle.

Heloïse (f)
Old French, revived in nineteenth century.
Variant Eloïse.
Famous name Heloise, the ill-fated lover of the twelfth-century abbot, Abelard.

Henry (m)
Norman, meaning 'home ruler'.
Variants Henery, Henri, Henrik.
Diminutives Harry, Hal, Hank, Herry.
Feminine Henrietta, Henryetta, Heneretta, Harriet etc.
Diminutives Hetty, Henny, Etta.
Famous names Eight kings of England; Henry Kissinger, American peace negotiator; Henry Cooper, boxer; Henry James, novelist; Hank Wangford, R & B singer.

Herb (m)
See Herbert.

Herbert (m)
Norman of Germanic origin, meaning 'famous army'.
Diminutives Herb, Herbie.

Herman (m)
Old German, meaning 'soldier'.
Variant Armand (French).

Hermione (f)
Greek from Hermes, who was the messenger of the gods.
Famous names Hermione, wife of King Leontes in Shakespeare's play *The Winter's Tale*; Hermione Gingold, British actress.

Hester (f)
See Esther.

Hettie (f)
See Henrietta, under Henry.

Hilary (m,f)
Latin, meaning 'cheerful'.
Variants Hillary, Hillery.

Hilda (f)
Northern European, from Old Teutonic meaning 'my support'.
Famous name Saint Hilda, Northumbrian princess who founded Whitby Abbey.

Holly (f)
Twentieth-century English, named after the evergreen tree.
Variant Hollie.

Honey (f)
Twentieth-century English, it became popular after the film version of Margaret Mitchell's *Gone with the Wind*, in which she is a character.

Honor (f)
Latin, meaning 'honour'.
Variants Honora, Honoria, Honour, Honorine.
Famous name Honor Blackman, English actress.

Hope (f)
One of the virtues.
Variants Esperance, Esperanza.
Famous name One of the main characters in the TV series, *Thirty Something*.

Horace (m)
From the Roman clan name.
Variant Horatio.
Feminine Horatia.
Famous name Nelson, English naval commander.

Howard (m)
Surname used as first name, possibly meaning 'heart's guardian'.
Famous name Howard Hughes, millionaire businessman, film director, aviator and eccentric.

Hubert (m)
Germanic origin, meaning 'bright spirit'.

Hugh (m)
Old German, meaning 'heart' or 'spirit'.
Variants Huw (Welsh), Hugo.
Famous name Hugh Grant, popular English actor.

Hywel (m)
Welsh, meaning 'eminent'. Very popular.
Famous name Hywel Bennett, TV actor.

I

Ian (m)
Scottish form of John.
Variant Iain.
Famous names Iain Banks, novelist best known for *The Wasp Factory* and *Complicity*; Ian Botham, English cricketer; Ian Rush, Welsh footballer; Ian Fleming, creator of the James Bond novels.

Ianthe (f)
Greek, meaning 'violet flower'.

Ida (f)
Norman, of Germanic origin.
Famous name Princess Ida, opera by Gilbert and Sullivan, based on Alfred, Lord Tennyson's poem, 'The Princess', of which Ida was the heroine.

Idris (m)
Welsh medieval, meaning 'ardent lord', now enjoying a revival.

Ifor (m)
Welsh, of uncertain origin.

Ike (m)
See Isaac.

Immanuel (m)
See Emanuel.

Imogen (f)
Of disputed origin, possibly from the Latin *innocens*, meaning 'innocent' or the Celtic, *ingean*, meaning 'maiden'.
Famous names Imogen Stubbs, television and film actress; Imogen Holst, composer and pianist.

Ines, Inez (f)
See Agnes.

Inga (f)
Old Norse, referring to a fertility god; short for Ingeborg.
Variant Inge.

Ingrid (f)
Old Norse, meaning 'beautiful'.
Famous name Ingrid Bergman, Oscar-winning actress.

Inigo (m)
Form of Ignatius, uncertain origin.

Innes (m,f)
Scottish variation of Angus.

Iola (f)
Greek, meaning 'dawn cloud'.

Iona (f)
Scottish and English, name of island sanctuary off Scottish coast.

Ira (m)
Hebrew meaning 'watchful'. Biblical but still in use in the United States.

Irene (f)
Latin, meaning 'peace'.
Variant Irena.
Famous names Soames's wife in *The Forsyte Saga* by John Galsworthy; Irene Handl, comic actress.

Iris (f)
Greek, meaning 'rainbow', but also referring to flower.
Famous name Iris Murdoch, English novelist.

Irma (f)
Similar origin to Emma.
Famous name Irma la Douce, musical.

Irvin (m)
From the surname and Scottish place name.
Variants Irvine, Irving.
Famous name Irving Berlin, American composer and lyricist.

Irwin (m)
See Irvin.

Isaac (m)
Hebrew, meaning 'laughter'.
Variant Izaak.
Diminutives Zac, Zachary.
Famous name Isaac Israel Hayes, American Arctic explorer and author.

Isbel (f)
See Isabel.

Isabel (f)
Spanish version of Elizabeth.
Variants Isabella, Isobel, Isbel, Ishbel.
Diminutive Izzy.
Famous names Isabella Rossellini, actress, model and the 'face' of cosmetics' company *Lancome; Isabella, or The Pot of Basil* is a narrative poem by John Keats (1818).

Isidore (m)
Greek, meaning 'gift of Isis'.
Variants Isador, Isidor, Dore, Dorian, Dory, Izzy.
Feminine Isidora, Isadora.
Famous name Isadora Duncan, American dancer.

Isla (f)
Scottish of recent origin (first part pronounced as in Isle).
Famous name Isla Sinclair, television hostess.

Isolde (f)
Probably from Old Welsh, meaning 'fair'.
Variants Ysolde, Yesult, Isolte, Yseulte, Isolda.

Iva (f)
Feminine of Ivan.
Variant Ivana.
Famous name Ivana Trump, novelist and ex-wife of Donald Trump, the hotel and gambling magnate.

Ivan (m)
Russin form of John.
Feminine Ivanna, Ivana.
Dimunitive Vanya (m).
Famous name Ivan the Terrible, Russia's first Tsar.

Ivo (m)
Variation of French Yves.
Variant Ivon.
Famous name Ivon Hutchins, English painter.

Ivor (m)
Old Norse, meaning 'yew' and 'warrior'.
Famous name Ivor Gurney, First World War poet.

Ivy (f)
Victorian name, based on plant.
Famous name Ivy Compton-Burnett, novelist.

J

Jacinta (f)
Spanish form of Greek, meaning 'hyacinth'.
Variant Jacinthe (French).

Jack (m)
Originally a diminutive of John, now a name in its own right.
Famous names Jack London, writer; Jack Kerouac, Beat poet; Jack Nicholson, actor.

Jackie (m,f)
As a female name, a diminutive of Jacqueline.

Jackson (m)
English, originally surname.

Jacob (m)
Hebrew, meaning 'one who supplants'.
Feminine Jacobina, Jacoba.
Diminutive Jake.

Jacqueline (f)
French, feminine of Jacques (see James).

Variants Jackeline, Jaclyn, Jacquelyn, Jaqueline.
Famous names Jackie Onassis, American First Lady; Jacqueline Dupré, cellist.

Jacquetta (f)
English respelling of Italian Giachetta.
Diminutives Jackie, Jacqui.
Famous name Jacquetta Hawkes, writer.

Jacqui (f)
See Jacqueline.

Jade (f)
Recent English, from the precious stone.
Famous name Mick Jagger, rock star, named his daughter Jade.

Jago (m)
Cornish and Welsh variant of James.
Variant Iago.

Jake (m).
See Jacob.

James (m)
From Jacob, 'one who supplants'.
Variants Seamus (Irish), Hamish (Scottish), Jacques (French), Jaime (Spanish).
Diminutives Jem, Jim, Jimmy, Jamie.
Feminine Jametta, Jamelia, Jamila, Jamie.
Famous names James VI, who became king of Scotland in 1567, at the age of one year and one month; Jim Davidson, comedian; James Joyce, Irish writer; James Ensor, Belgian artist; James Cameron, news reporter and journalist; James Callaghan, British prime minister.

Jamie (m)
See James.

Jana (f)
Form of Jane in Central Europe.

Jancis (f)
Modern English combination of Jan and Frances.
Famous name Jancis Robinson, television wine buff.

Jane (f)
Feminine spelling of John, from Latin, Johanna.
Variants Jaine, Jayne, Janene, Sine.
Gaelic variants Sheena, Sheenagh, Sheona.
Famous name Jayne Torvill, ice dance champion; Jane Austen, English novelist; *Jane Eyre*, novel by Charlotte Brontë; Jane Asher, English actress; Jane Lapotaire, actress.

Janet (f)
Variant of Jane.
Variants Janette, Jenette, Jenetta, Janetta, Janice, Janis.
Famous name Janis Joplin, jazz singer.

Janey (f)
See Jane.

Janice (f)
See Janet.

Janine (f)
English version of French Jeannine.

Jared (m)
Hebrew, meaning 'to descend'.

Jarvis (m)
See Gervase.

Jasmine (f)
From the flower.
Variants Jessamine, Jessamy, Yasmin, Yasmina.
Famous name Yasmin le Bon, international model and wife of pop star Simon le Bon.

Jason (m)
Greek, mythical leader of the Argonauts who underwent many hardships and adventures in their quest for the Golden Fleece. Recently it has become a very popular name for boys and for labrador dogs.

Jasper (m)
English of Persian origin, meaning 'treasurer', and supposedly the name of one of the three wise men.
Variants Caspar, Gaspard.

Jay (m,f)
Diminutive of any name beginning with J.

Jayne (f)
Variant of Jane.

Jean (f)
Feminine form of John.
Variants Jeanne, Jeane, Jeannette, Jeanine, Jeanetta, Jeannie, Jeannine, Jehan.
Masculine Jean (French form of John)
Famous names Jeanne d'Arc, French girl martyr; Jean Muir, fashion designer; Jean Cocteau, French writer.

Jed (m)
American, short for Biblical name Jedidiah, but now a name in its own right.

Jeff (m)
Diminutive of Jeffrey, but now used in its own right.

Jeffrey (m)
See Geoffrey.

Jemima (f)
Hebrew, meaning 'dove'.

Jenni (f)
Modern form of Jenny, see Jennifer.

Jennifer (f)
Welsh, meaning 'fair and smooth'.
Variants Guinevere, Gaynor, Gweniver, Jenifer.
Diminutives Jen, Jenney, Jennie, Jenny (originally derived from Janet).
Famous names Guinevere, the wife of King Arthur in Arthurian legend; Jenny Seagrove, English actress; Jennifer Saunders, comedienne.

Jeremy (m)
Biblical, English version of Jeremiah.
Diminutives Jerry, Jem.
Famous names Jeremy Paxman, writer and television presenter; Jeremy Irons, English actor.

Jerome (m)
Anglicized version of Hieronymos, meaning 'holy name'.
Diminutives Jerry.
Famous names Saint Jerome made the first Latin translation of the Bible; Jerome K. Jerome, author of *Three Men in a Boat*.

Jesse (m)
Hebrew, meaning 'Jehovah exists'.

Jessica (f)
Hebrew, meaning 'he beholds'.
Famous name Jessica Mitford, writer.

Jessie (f)
Diminutive of Jean (Scottish) and Jessica.

Jethro (m)
From Hebrew, meaning 'excellence'.
Famous names Jethro Tull, eighteenth-century agricultural reformer; 'Jethro Tull', rock group.

Jill (f)
Diminutive of Gillian, but used in its own right.
Famous name Jill Bennett, actress.

Jillian (f)
See Gillian.

Jim (m)
See James.

Jimmy (m)
See James.

Jinny (f)
Diminutive of Virginia (also Ginny), Jane or Jenny, sometimes used independently.

Jo (f,m)
Diminutive of Joanna, Josephine and Joseph.

Joan (f)
English version of Old French Johanne.
Diminutives Joanie, Joni.
Famous names Joan Baez, folk singer; Joan Sutherland, Australian opera singer.

Joanna (f)
Feminine form of Johannes (John).
Variants Joanne, Johanna, Jo Anna, Joannah, Jo-Ann.
Diminutives Jo, Jojo, Joey.
Famous name Joanna Lumley, English actress.

Job (m)
Biblical, meaning 'persecuted'.
Variants Joby, Jobie.

Jocasta (f)
English, from Greek legend, where Jocasta was the mother of Oedipus.
Famous name Jocasta Innes expert in painting and decorative techniques.

Jocelyn (m,f)
From the Norman, once a boy's name, now more commonly a girl's.

Jock (m)
Scottish variant of Jack.

Jodie (f)
See Judith.
Variants Jodi, Jody.
Famous name Jodie Foster, film actress.

Joe, Joey (m)
Diminutive of Joseph.

Joel (m)
Hebrew, meaning God (twice over).

Joelle (f)
French.

John (m)
Hebrew, meaning 'God has been gracious'.
Variants Sion, Evan (Welsh), Sean (Irish), Ivan, Vanya (Russian), Ian (Scottish), Jan (European).
Diminutives Johnny, Johnnie, Jack.
Feminine Vania (from Russian Vanya).
Famous names John Cleese, actor and comedian; John Major, British prime minister; Jon Snow, television news reporter; John Snow, cricketer; John Masefield, poet laureate; John Betjeman, poet laureate; John Lennon, pop star; John the Baptist; John Osborne, author of *Look Back in Anger*; John Mortimer, author; the popular Pope John XXIII; John Cage, composer.

Johnny (m)
Diminutive of John.

Jolene (f)
New name which appeared in the 1940s.
Variants Jolinda, Joleen, Jolean.
Famous name Dolly Parton's song *Jolene.*

Jon (m)
Swedish form of John.

Jonathan (m)
Hebrew, meaning 'God has given'.
Variant Johnathan.
Diminutive Jon.
Famous names Jonathan Swift, author of the satirical *Gulliver's Travels;* Jonathan Aitken, member of Parliament; Jonathan Dimbleby, television journalist.

Joni (f)
Modern form of Jon.

Variant Jonni.
Famous name Joni Mitchell, Canadian-born singer and song-writer.

Jonquil (f)
From the flower, introduced in the mid-twentieth century.
Variant Jonquille.

Jordan (m)
Hebrew, meaning 'to descend', sometimes used as a girl's name.

Joseph (m)
Hebrew, meaning 'God adds'.
Famous names Joseph Grimaldi, great pantomime clown; Saint Joseph of Arimathea who, legend has it, when imprisoned for twelve years, was kept alive by the Holy Grail; Joseph Conrad, Polish author who wrote *Lord Jim* and *Heart of Darkness*.

Josephine (f)
Feminine form of Joseph.
Variants Josephina, Josephene, Josette.
Diminutive Josie (used independently).
Famous names Josephine, wife of French Emperor, Napoleon Bonaparte; Jo Brand, comedienne.

Josh (m)
Diminutive of Joshua, sometimes used in its own right.

Joshua (m)
Hebrew, meaning 'the Lord is salvation'.
Diminutive Josh (used independently).
Famous name Joshua Reynolds, painter.

Joss (m)
Diminutive of Jocelyn.

Joy (f)
Noun used as a name.
Variants Joye, Joi, Joya.

Joyce (m,f)
Celtic, derived from Jesse.

Juanita (f)
Spanish feminine of Juan (John).
Variants Janita, Junita.

Jude (m)
Diminutive of Judas.
Famous names Thomas Hardy's novel, *Jude the Obscure*; Beatles song 'Hey Jude'.

Judith (f)
Hebrew, meaning 'Jewess'.
Diminutives Judy (used independently), Jodie, Jody.
Famous name Dame Judy Dench, English actress.

Jules (m)
Form of Julius.
Variant Jools.
Famous name Jools Holland, musician and television presenter.

Julia (f)
Feminine form of Julius.
Variants Julie, Juliet, Juliette.

Julian (m)
From Julius.
Variants Julien, Julion, Jolyon.

Juliana (f)
Feminine form of Julian.
Variants Julianne, Liane, Lianne, Lianna, Julie-Anne, Juliane.

Julie (f)
French variant of Julia.
Famous names Julie Andrews, actress; Julie Christie, actress.

Juliet (f)
English variation of Italian Giulietta.
Variant Juliette.
Famous name Shakespeare's *Romeo and Juliet*.

June (f)
Twentieth-century English name.
Famous name June Whitfield, actress and comedienne.

Juno (f)
Celebrated deity among the ancients, she was regarded as the divine prototype of wife and mother and the special patroness of marriage.

Justin (m)
Latin, meaning'just'.
Variant Justyn.
Feminine Justine, Justina.
Famous name *Justine*, one of Lawrence Durrell's novels in the Alexandria Quartet.

K

Kai (f)
Hawaiian word for 'sea', variant of Kay, possibly a diminutive of Kylie.
Variants Ky, Kye.

Kane (m)
Welsh, meaning 'beautiful'. Popular in Australia since the 1960s.

Karen (f)
Diminutive of Katarina, introduced by Danish settlers to the United States.
Variants Karan, Karena, Karina, Karon, Karyn, Caren, Carin, Carina, Caron, Caronne, Caryn.
Famous names Karen Carpenter, American singer who together with her brother Richard formed the successful singing duo, 'The Carpenters'; Karen Blixen, Danish writer who used the pseudonym 'Isaac Dimesen'.

Karenza (f)
Cornish, meaning 'love'.
Variants Kerensa, Kerenza.

Karl (m)
See Carl.

Kate (f)
Diminutive of Katherine.

Katerina (f)
Russian variant of Katherine.

Kath (f)
Diminutive of Katherine.

Katherine (f)
Greek, meaning 'pure' (see also Catherine).
Variants Katharine, Kathryn, Katarina, Kathleen, Katarine, Katia, Katya, Katinka, Katrina, Katrine, Karen, Karran, Karren, Karyn.
Diminutives Kate, Katey, Katie, Kay, Kitty, Kath, Kathy, Kathe, Katy.
Famous names St Katharine of Alexandria; several saints and Queens of England; Katherine Mansfield, New Zealand novelist and short story writer; Kathryn Hepburn, American actress; Kate Bush, pop singer.

Kay (f)
Diminutive of names beginning K, used independently.
Variant Kaye.

Kayley (f)
Recent Irish and English, or uncertain origin.
Variants Kayly, Kayleigh.

Keir (m)
Gaelic, meaning 'swarthy'.

Keith (m)
Scottish from place in East Lothian meaning 'wood'.
Feminine variant Keitha.
Famous name Keith Richards, member of the 'Rolling Stones' pop group.

Kelly (f)
From the Irish surname, possibly meaning 'strife'.
Variants Kealey, Kayley, Kaylee, Kiley, Kelley, Keighley, Keiley, Kylie, Kylee.

Kelvin (m)
Celtic, from the river name.
Variant Kelvyn.
Famous name Kelvin Grant, reggae performer with the band 'Musical Youth'.

Ken (m)
Diminutive of Kenneth.

Kennedy (m)
Irish, Scottish and English, from Gaelic meaning 'ugly head'. Recently used in memory of John F. Kennedy, the American president assassinated in 1963.

Kenneth (m)
Gaelic, meaning 'fair and fiery'.
Diminutives Ken, Kenny.
Feminine Kennice, Kenia, Kena, Kenza.
Famous names Kenneth Branagh, English actor; Kenneth Grahame, author of *Wind in the Willows*; Ken Loach, film director; Kenny Everett, the late DJ and comedian.

Kenny (m)
See Kenneth.

Kent (m)
Recent English, probably named after county.

Kenton (m)
Originally English surname.
Famous name Sheila's twin in BBC Radio soap, *The Archers*.

Kerry (f,m)
Australian, probably named after Irish county.
Famous name Kerry Packer, Australian entrepreneur.

Kevin (m)
Irish, meaning 'born handsome'.
Famous names Kevin Costner, American actor and director; Kevin Keegan, footballer.

Kieran (m)
Irish, meaning 'dark'. From Gaelic Ciaran.
Variant Kyran.
Famous name Kieran Bracken, Rugby footbll player.

Kim (f,m)
Diminutive of Kimberley.
Famous name Kim Novak, film actress.

Kimberley (m,f)
From the 'diamond' town in S. Africa.
Variants Kimberly, Kimberlyn (f), Kimberlee, Kimbley.
Diminutives Kim, Kimba (f).

Kingsley (m)
English, from the place name meaning 'wood of the king'.
Famous name Kingsley Amis, poet and novelist whose first novel, *Lucky Jim*, achieved popular success.

Kirk (m)
Old Norse, meaning 'church'.
Famous name Kirk Douglas, American actor and father of actor Michael Douglas.

Kirsten (f)
Form of Christine.
Variants Kerstine, Kirstin, Kirstyn.
Diminutives Kirstie, Kirsti, Kirsty.
Famous name Kirsten Flagstad, Norwegian soprano.

Kit (m)
Diminutive of Christopher, sometimes used independently.

Kitty (f)
Diminutive of Katherine.

Kurt (m)
Diminutive of Konrad but now used in its own right.
Famous name Kurt Jurgens, film actor.

Kylie (f)
Aboriginal, meaning 'throwing stick'.
Famous name Kylie Minogue, Australian actress and singer.

L

Lachlan (m)
Gaelic, meaning 'land of lochs'.

Lakeisha (f)
Example of the recently popular practice among African–American parents of prefixing girls' names with La.
Variants Lakisha, Ladonna, Ladiva, Lanetta, Lashawna, Latanya, Laoia, Ladonna.

Lana (f)
Latin, meaning'wool', diminutive of Alana.
Famous name Lana Turner, American film actress.

Lance (m)
Diminutive of Lancelot.

Lancelot (m)
Either from Latin, meaning 'little lance or warrior', or from Celtic, meaning 'territory'. Best known as one of King Arthur's knights, who fell in love with Queen Guinevere.
Diminutive Lance.

Famous name Lance Percival, actor, singer and entertainer.

Lara (f)
Possibly a diminutive of Italian Larisa, or Russian Larissa.
Famous name Lara was popularized as an independent name by the character in the film *Dr Zhivago.*

Larissa (f)
Russian, origin uncertain: either the name of a Greek martyr, or Latin, meaning 'cheerful'.

Larry (m)
Diminutive of Laurence or Lawrence. An independent name since the beginning of this century.
Famous name Larry Grayson, television host.

Laura (f)
Latin, meaning 'laurel'.
Variants Laureen, Laurice, Laurine, Lorene, Laurel, Lauren, Laurena, Lorinda, Lorene, Lorina, Laurette, Lauretta, Loretta, Lorretta, Laurianne, Lori Ann, Lora, Lorin.
Diminutives Lauri, Lory, Lori, Lorri.
Famous name Lauren Bacall, American actress and widow of screen legend, Humphrey Bogart.

Laurence (m)
Latin from the town that took its name from the laurel plant.
Variants Lawrence, Lars (Swedish), Laurance, Loren, Lorenzo.
Diminutives Larry, Laurie, Lawrie.
Famous names T. E. Lawrence, known as Lawrence of Arabia; Laurence Olivier, actor, director and producer;

Saint Lawrence, whose feast is celebrated on 10 August is the patron saint of curriers. He was martyred in 258 by being roasted on a grid-iron.

Lavender (f)
English name favoured in Victorian times, taken from the scented plant.

Lavinia (f)
Latin, meaning 'of Latium'. There is a coastal town called Lavinia south of Rome. In myth Lavinia was the wife of Aeneas, and therefore mother of the Romans.

Lawson (m)
English surname, popular as a first name since the middle of the nineteenth century.

Leah (f)
Hebrew, meaning 'languid'.
This is a biblical name mentioned in the Book of Genesis.
Variant Lea.

Lee (m,f)
Old English, meaning 'gentle being', and surname meaning 'wood' or 'clearing', used as a first name from the early part of this century.
Feminine Lea, Lee Ann, Leeann, Leigh Ann, Lianne.
Famous names Lee Majors, the 'Six-Million Dollar Man'; Lee Harvey Oswald, John F. Kennedy's assassin, Lee Dorsey, American rhythm 'n' blues singer.

Leigh (m,f)
Anglo-Saxon, meaning 'wayside beauty'.
Also variant of Lee.

Leila (f)
Arabic, meaning 'dark as night'.
Variants Layla, Lela, Leilah, Lilah.
Famous name Eric Clapton, singer and songwriter, dedicated his song *Layla* to George Harrison's wife. Clapton later married her and the song has become a classic.

Len (m)
Diminutive of Leonard, or occasionally Lionel.
Famous name Len Murray, trade union leader.

Lena (f)
Diminutive of Helena or used in its own right.
Famous name Lena Horne, American singer.

Lennard (m)
See Leonard.

Lennox (m)
Scottish surname, based on a place, Levenach.
Famous name Lennox Berkeley, composer.

Lenny (m)
Diminutive of Len, Leonard.
Famous name Lenny Bruce, American comedian.

Lenora (f)
See Leonora.

Leo (m)
Greek, meaning 'lion'. Leo is the first sign of the Zodiac, representing the period from 23 July to 22 August.
Variant Leon.
Feminine Leona, Leonie.
Famous name Leo Sayer, singer/songwriter.

Leonard (m)
Old German, meaning 'strong as a lion'.
Famous names Leonardo da Vinci, Italian painter, sculptor and architect; Leonard Bernstein, American composer, conductor, author and pianist; Leonard Rossiter, actor.

Leonie (f)
See Leonard.

Leonora (f)
Diminutive of Eleonora, now used in its own right.

Leopold (m)
Germanic, meaning 'bold people'.
Diminutive Leo.
Famous name King Leopold of the Belgians, uncle of Queen Victoria.

Leroy (m)
American, from Old French 'le roy', meaning 'the king'.

Leslie (m,f)
Scottish surname and place name, possibly meaning 'garden of hollies'.
Variant Lesley.
Feminine Lesley, Leslie.
Famous name Leslie Charteris, crime and adventure novelist, creator of 'The Saint'.

Lester (m)
Originally surname, based on town of Leicester.
Famous name Lester Piggott, jockey.

Lew (m)
Diminutive of Lewis.
Famous name Lew Grade, television entrepreneur.

Lewin (m)
Old English, meaning 'beloved friend'.

Lewis (m)
Diminutive of Llewelyn, also a variant of Louis.
Famous name Lewis Carroll, much-loved English author and mathematician.

Liam (m)
Diminutive of William, used as an independent name, particularly in Ireland.

Libby (f)
Diminutive of Elizabeth, now sometimes used in its own right.
Famous name Libby Purves, television and radio presenter.

Lili (f)
German diminutive of Elizabeth.
Variant Lilli.
Famous name 'Lili Marlene', popular song of the Second World War.

Lilian (f)
Latin, meaning 'lily'.
Variants Liliana, Lily, Lilia, Lilley, Lilly.
Famous name Lillian Gish, American silent screen actress.

Lina (f)
Diminutive of names ending in 'lina', Angelina, Emelina, Carolina. Now used as an independent name.

Linda (f)
Associated with Spanish, meaning 'pretty', but probably originated as a diminutive of names ending 'linda', Belinda, Melinda, Rosalinda. Popular in the period between World War 1 and World War 2.
Variants Lyn, Lynne Lynne, Lynda.
Diminutives Lindy, Lyndi.
Famous names Linda Blair, American actress who was nominated for an Academy award for her portrayal of a possessed girl in the film, *The Exorcist* (1973); Linda McCartney, vegetarian cookery writer, and wife of Paul, member of the Beatles; Lynn Fontaine, ballet dancer.

Lindsay (m,f)
Originally a Scottish surname and then a boy's name. By the middle of this century it had become more popular as a girl's name.
Variants Lindsey, Lynsey, Lyndsey, Linsay.

Lionel (m)
Greek, meaning 'little lion'.
Famous names Lionel Barrymore, part of the great Barrymore acting family and great uncle of popular teen actress, Drew Barrymore; Lionel Blue, rabbi, cook and humorist; Lionel Hampton, American jazz musician.

Lis (f)
Diminutive of Elisabeth.

Lisa (f)
Diminutive of Elisabeth.
Famous name Lisa Minelli.

Lisbet (f)
Diminutive of Elisabeth, sometimes used in its own right.

Lisette (f)
French, diminutive of Elisabeth.

Lizzie (f)
Diminutive of Elizabeth.

Livia (f)
Latin, a famous Roman lady, mother of Emperor Tiberius. Also diminutive of Olivia.

Liza (f)
Diminutive of Elisabeth.

Llewelyn (m)
Welsh, meaning 'lionlike' or 'leader'.
Variants Llewllyn, Lewellen.

Lloyd (m)
Welsh, meaning 'grey'.
Variant Loyd.

Lois (f)
New Testament name, no relation to Louise.

Lola (f)
Diminutive of Dolores.
Famous name Lola Montez, mistress of the composer Liszt and writer Alexander Dumas.

Lolita (f)
See Dolores.

Lonnie (m)
English or uncertain origin. Possibly corruption of Lenny.
Famous name Lonnie Donegan, rock 'n' roll singer.

Lorna (f)
Scottish, from the place name, 'Lorn'.
Variants Lorn, Lorne (the latter sometimes used for boys).
Famous name Popularized by R. D. Blackmore's novel, *Lorna Doone* (1869).

Lorraine (f)
Scottish surname from the French province, possibly first used during the rule of Mary Queen of Scots whose mother was Mary of Lorraine. Could also be a variant of Lora.
Variants Loraine, Lorain, Lorane, Lorayne.

Lottie (f)
Diminutive of Charlotte.
Variant Lotty.

Lou (m,f)
Diminutive of Louis or Louise.

Louella (f)
Modern English, made up from Louise and Ella.
Variant Luella.

Louis (m)
French from the Old German, meaning 'fame in war'.
Variants Lewis, Luis, Ludwig, Ludovic.
Feminine Louisa, Louise, Louiza, Luisa.
Famous names Louis Braille who, blind from the age of three, invented raised-point reading in 1854; Louis Wain, cat artist.

Louise (f)
Feminine form of Louis.
Variants Louisa, Louiza, Luisa.
Diminutives Lou, Lulu, Lula.
Famous names Louisa M. Alcott, author of *Little Women*; Lulu, pop singer.

Loveday (f)
Cornish name, origin unknown, but still in use.

Lucas (m)
Latin, from the place name, 'Lucania'.
Diminutive Luke (used independently).

Lucia (f)
Part of a Roman name meaning 'light'.
Variants Luce, Lucy, Lucetta, Lucilla, Lucille, Lucinda.
Masculine Lucian, Lucien.
Famous name Lucille Ball, actress, known for her 'I Love Lucy' shows; Lucinda Lambton, journalist and social historian.

Lucy (f)
See Lucia.

Ludo (m)
Diminutive of Ludovic.

Ludovic (m)
English and Scottish, anglicized from Gaelic name meaning 'devoted to the Lord'.
Diminutive Ludo.
Famous name Ludovic Kennedy, journalist and writer.

Luke (m)
English, deriving from Lucas, which in turn came from Greek, meaning 'the man fom Lucani'.

Variant Jean-Luc (French).
Famous names Saint Luke, patron saint of artists and physicians, whose feast day is on 18 October; Jean-Luc Goddard, film director.

Lulu (f)
See Louise.

Luther (m)
Old German, comprised of 'people' and 'army'.
Variants Lothair, Lothario (meaning 'famous').
Famous names Martin Luther, German leader of the Protestant Reformation; Martin Luther King Jr, American civil rights campaigner.

Lydia (f)
Greek, meaning 'woman of Lydia'.

Lyndon (m)
English surname, became popular around the time of World War 1.
Famous name Lyndon Johnson, US president.

Lynette (f)
Derived from Celtic, Luned. May also be a fancy spelling of the bird, linnet.

Lynn (f)
Modern English diminutive of Linda.

Lynton (m)
Place name, from the River Lyn.
Variant Linton.

Lys (f)
See Elizabeth.

Lysette (f)
Variant of Lisette.

M

Mabel (f)
Diminutive of Amabel, French, meaning 'my beauty'.
Variants Mabelle, Maybell, Mable.
Famous name Mabel Lucy Attwell, children's writer and illustrator.

Madeleine (f)
Hebrew, meaning 'woman of Magdala'; birthplace of the biblical Mary Magdalene.
Variants Madeline, Madaleine, Magdalene, Magdalena, Magdelina, Madelina, Malena, Malina.
Diminutives Magda, Lena.
Famous name Madeleine Bejart, the first of France's professional actresses.

Madonna (f)
Italian, from the title of the Virgin Mary.
Famous name Madonna (Ciccone), American popular singer.

Mae (f)
Variant of May.

Famous name Mae West, American film star, who gave name to an inflatable life jacket.

Maeve (f)
Irish, from Celtic name meaning 'inducing intoxication' and mentioned in Celtic epic tale 'The Cattle Raid of Cooley'.
Variants Mave, Meave.
Famous name Maeve Binchy, popular Irish novelist.

Magda (f)
German and Czech name, diminutive of Magdalena.

Maggie (f)
Diminutive of Margaret.
Famous name Maggie Smith, actress.

Magnus (m)
Latin, meaning 'great'.
Variants Manus, Magnes, Manius.
Famous name Magnus Magnusson, television presenter.

Mahala (f)
Hebrew, meaning 'tenderness'.
Variants Mahlah, Mahalia, Mehala, Mehalia.

Mai (f)
Swedish, diminutive of Maria.
Famous name Mai Zetterling, film actress and producer.

Mairona (f)
Diminutive of Irish Mary.

Maisie (f)
Scottish diminutive of Mairead, Gaelic for Margaret.
Famous name Henry James's novel, *What Maisie Knew*.

Malachy (m)
Irish name of king who routed Norse invaders. Malachi is also one of the prophets in the Old Testament.
Variant Malachi.

Malcolm (m)
Scottish, derived from Gaelic name meaning 'disciple of (Saint) Columbus'.
Diminutive Calum.
Famous names Sir Malcolm Sargent, conductor; Malcolm Lowry, novelist, author of *Under the Volcano*; Malcolm Bradbury, novelist.

Manfred (m)
German and English, meaning 'man of peace'.
Famous names Byron's epic poem, 'Manfred'; Manfred Mann, pop singer.

Mandy (f)
Diminutive of Amanda, used independently.

Manny (m)
Diminutive of Emmanuel.

Mara (f)
Hebrew, meaning 'bitter'.

Marc (f)
French variation of Mark.
Famous names Marc Bolan, pop singer; Marc Chagall, Russian painter.

Marcel (f)
Form of the Latin name Marcus.
Feminine Marcelle, Marcella, Marcene.

Famous names Marcel Marceau, French mime artist; Marcel Proust, writer of *In Remembrance of Times Past*; Marcel Pagnal, author of *Manon des Sources*.

Marcia (f)
From Mars, the Roman god of war.
Variant Marsha.
Diminutives Marcy, Marci(e).

Marcus (m)
See Mark.

Margaret (f)
Greek, meaning 'pearl'.
Variants Margarita, Marguerite, Margherita, Margot, Margo, Margret, Margurite, Marjory, Marjorie, Margery.
Diminutives Madge, Maggie, Meg, Megan, Maisie, Greta, Gretchen, Peggy.
Famous names Princess Margaret, sister of Queen Elizabeth II; Margaret, now Baroness Thatcher; Margaret Atwood, Canadian novelist; Dame Peggy Ashcroft, actress; Dame Margot Fonteyn, ballerina; Marguerite Duras, French writer.

Maria (f)
The Latin form of Mary.
Variants Marie, Mari, Mariel, Marielle, Mariella, Marietta, Mariam, Miriam.
Famous names Marie Curie, world-famous scientist and discoverer of the element radium; Marie Stopes, pioneer of contraception for women; Maria Callas, opera singer.

Marian (f)
From Marie.

Variants Marion, Marianne, Mariana, Mariane, Mary-Ann(e).
Famous name Marianne Faithfull, sixties wild-child and one time girlfriend of Mick Jagger.

Marigold (f)
English late nineteenth-century name, based on the pungent orange flower, so called in honour of the Virgin Mary. Marigold also meant a sovereign in seventeenth-century slang.

Marika (f)
Slavonic diminutive of Maria, used in its own right.
Famous name Marika Hanbury-Tennison, cookery writer.

Marilyn (f)
Combination of the names Mary and Ellen.
Variants Marillyn, Maralin, Marolyn, Marylin, Marylyn, Marylina.
Famous name Marilyn Monroe, the most celebrated of all screen goddesses.

Marina (f)
English, Spanish and Italian. May be the feminine form of Marinus, or might mean 'little Mary'.
Famous name Marina Warner, writer.

Marion (m,f)
English, used either for male or female.

Mark (m)
From Mars, the Roman god of war.
Variants Marc, Marcus, Mario, Marius.
Famous names Saint Mark, one of the gospel writers, whose feast day falls on 25 April; King Mark of Cornwall, who lived at Tintagel, and whose wife was

the tragic Ysolde who fell in love with Tristram; Mark Spitz, swimmer.

Marlene (f)
Combination of the names Maria and Magdalene.
Variants Marla, Marleen, Marlena, Marlyn.
Diminutives Marley, Marlee.
Famous name Marlene Dietrich, film actress.

Marlon (m)
Of uncertain origin, popularized by actor Marlon Brando.

Marmaduke (m)
Irish, of uncertain origin.
Diminutive Duke.

Martha (f)
Aramaic, meaning 'lady of the house'.
Variants Marta (Italian), Marthe (French).
Diminutives Marti, Marty, Matty.
Famous names The 'Marthas' were the women who cleaned and cooked in Margaret Atwood's futuristic novel, *The Handmaid's Tale*; Martha Graham, dancer and choreographer.

Marshall (m)
English from surname, originally meaning someone who looked after horses.
Famous name Marshall McLuhan, advertising expert, who created the slogan 'The media is the message'.

Marti (f)
English diminutive of Martina.
Famous name Marti Caine, comedienne.

Martin (m)
Latin, meaning 'Martinus'.
Variant Martyn.
Feminine Martine, Martina.
Famous names Saint Martin, patron saint of innkeepers and reformed drunkards, whose feast day is 11 November; Martin Luther, protestant reformer; Martin Amis, novelist; Martina Navratilova, tennis ace.

Marvin (m)
Welsh, derived from the English name 'Merlin'.
Famous names Marvin Gaye, singer, composer, pianist and drummer, who was shot dead by his father during a quarrel; Marvin Hagler, boxer.

Mary (f)
One of the most popular names ever.
Variants Maria, Maire, Marya.
Diminutives May, Molly, Mia, Marika, Masha.
Famous names Mary Somerville, founder of the Oxford College; Mary McCarthy, American writer; *Mary Poppins*, musical; Mary O'Hara, Irish singer.

Matilda (f)
Norman, of Germanic origin, meaning 'might in battle'.
Diminutives Mattie, Tilly, Tillie.
Famous name Matilda, wife of William the Conqueror.

Matt (m)
See Matthew.

Matthew (m)
Hebrew, meaning 'gift of God'.
Variant Mathias.
Diminutive Matt, Mat.

Famous names Matt Busby, manager of Manchester United football club; Matt Dillon, American actor.

Maud (f)
English, medieval popular version of Matilda.
Famous names Alfred, Lord Tennyson's poem 'Maud', with the line 'Come into the garden, Maud'; Maud Gonne, a great beauty and Irish nationalist, much loved by the poet W B. Yeats.

Maura (f)
Celtic origin. Variation of Mary.
Famous name Saint Maura, fifth-century martyr.

Maureen (f)
Irish form of Mary.
Variants Maurene, Morine, Moreen.

Maurice (m)
Latin, meaning 'dark-skinned, a Moor'.
Variants Morris, Morice, Morriss.
Diminutive Moss (Irish, can be used independently).
Famous names Maurice Chevalier, French music hall artist; *Maurice*, novel by E. M. Forster; Maurice Ravel, composer.

Mavis (f)
Nineteenth-century invention, based on an Old French name for a song-thrush.
Diminutive Mave.

Max (m)
Diminutive for Maximilian.

Maxim (m)
Russian, from Latin, meaning 'the greatest'.
Famous name Maxim's, the celebrated restaurant.

Maximilian (m)
Latin, meaning 'the greatest'.
Variants Maxwell, Maxine, Maxime.
Diminutive Max (used independently).
Feminine Maxine, Maxima, Maxene, Maxina, Maxena.
Famous names Max Bygraves, British singer and comedian; Max Hastings, journalist; Max Beerbohm, critic, essayist and author of *Zuleika Dobson*.

Maxine (f)
Modern English, feminine version of Max.

May (f)
Diminutive of Mary and Margaret, but often used in its own right, based on the month and on hawthorn blossom.

Maya (f)
English anglicization of Roman goddess Maia, mother of Mercury.
Variant Maia.
Famous name Maya Angelou, black American writer (though in this case a nickname).

Maybelle (f)
Corruption of Mabel.

Maynard (m)
Originally a Norman surname, meaning 'brave strength'.
Famous name Maynard Keynes, economist.

Meg (f)
Diminutive of Margaret.

Megan (f)
Welsh diminutive of Meg, but used in its own right.
Variants Meghan, Meaghan.
Famous name Megan Lloyd George, first woman member of British Parliament.

Meggie (f)
Diminutive of Meg.

Melanie (f)
Greek, meaning 'dark-skinned'.
Variants Melane, Melani, Mellanie, Melonie, Melantha.

Melinda (f)
English, made up from combination of Melanie and Linda.

Melissa (f)
Greek, meaning 'bee'.
Variants Melisa, Mellissa.

Melita (f)
Latin, meaning 'honey sweet'.

Melody (f)
Recent English name, under influence of similar sounding names.

Melville (m)
French surname from place name.

Melvin (m)
Form of Melville, currently very popular.
Variant Melvyn.
Diminutive Mel.
Famous names Melvyn Bragg, novelist and television presenter; Mel Brooks, film director; Mel Gibson, Australian film actor/director.

Mercedes (f)
Spanish, meaning 'mercy'. Used by Catholic church to denote Our Lady of Mercies, celebrated on 10 August and 24 September.
Diminutives Mercy, Sadie (both used independently).

Mercy (f)
English, in use since seventeenth century.

Meredith (m,f)
Old Welsh name of uncertain origin.
Diminutive Merry.
Famous name Meredith, the female detective in Anne Granger's series of mystery novels.

Meriel (f)
Variant of Muriel.

Merle (f)
English, diminutive of Meriel, but used in its own right. Possibly related to Old French for 'blackbird'.
Famous name Merle Oberon, film actress.

Mervyn (m)
English version of Welsh Merfyn.
Variant Melvin.
Famous names Mervyn Peake, novelist, poet and artist; Mervyn Davies, Welsh rugby player.

Meryl (f)
Recent English.
Variant Melvin.
Famous name Meryl Streep, American actress.

Mia (f)
Diminutive of Maria.
Famous name Mia Farrow, American actress.

Michael (m)
Hebrew, meaning 'who is like the Lord?'.
Variants Michel, Mitchell, Michal, Mishka, Mischca.
Diminutives Mick, Mike, Mickey, Mickie, Mitch.
Feminine Michaela, Michelle, Michele.
Famous names Saint Michael, the archangel and leader of all the heavenly hosts, whose feast day, Michaelmas Day, is celebrated on 29 September; Michael Heseltine, British politician; 'Michelle', song by the Beatles; Michelle Pfeiffer, film actress; Mike Atherton, cricketer; Mick Hucknall, pop singer; Mike Aspel, television presenter; Mike Tyson, boxer; Mickey Rooney, American comedian, actor and singer; Mick Jagger, lead singer of the 'Rolling Stones'.

Mick (m)
See Michael.

Mike (m)
See Michael.

Mildred (f)
Victorian revival of Old English, meaning 'gentle strength'.
Famous name Seventh-century Saint Mildred was a daughter of Queen Ermenburh.

Miles (m)
Possibly Old German, meaning 'generous' or Slavic, meaning 'mercy'.
Variants Milo, Myles.
Famous name Miles Davis, jazz trumpeter and band-leader.

Millicent (f)
Norman, meaning 'strong worker'.

Diminutives Millie, Milly.
Famous name Millicent Martin, of TV series, *That Was The Week That Was.*

Mirabel (f)
Latin, meaning 'lovely, wondrous'. Used as a man's name in the seventeenth century.
Variants Mirabella, Mirabelle.

Miranda (f)
Latin, meaning 'admirable, to be admired'.
Diminutives Mandy, Mandi, Randy, Randi.
Famous name Prospero's daughter in Shakespeare's play, *The Tempest.*

Miriam (f)
Hebrew, from Maryam, the elder sister of Moses. Old form of Mary, probably originates from ancient Egypt.
Variants Mariam, Mariamme.
Diminutive Mitzi.
Famous name Miriam Margolyes, actress quoted as saying, 'Life, if you're fat, is a minefield - you have to pick your way, otherwise you blow up'.

Misha (m)
Russian diminutive for Michael.

Mitchell (m)
Derived from surname, which was a corruption of Michael.
Diminutive Mitch.

Mitzi (f)
Diminutive of Maria.

Moira (f)
Irish and Scottish, from Gaelic Maire.

Variation Moyra.
Famous name Moira Stewart, television newscaster.

Molly (f)
Diminutive of Mary.
Famous name 'Molly Malone', a traditional Irish song.

Mona *(f)*
From Gaelic, meaning 'noble'.

Monica (f)
Possibly from Greek, meaning 'alone' or Latin, meaning 'nun'.
Variant Monique.
Famous names Monica Dickens, granddaughter of novelist Charles Dickens and herself a prolific writer; Monica Seles, tennis player; Monique Wittig, experimental French novelist.

Montague (m)
Surname from French place name.
Variants Montagu, Monty.

Morag (f)
Scottish, from Gaelic. Now very popular.

Morgan (m,f)
Welsh, meaning 'great'.
Famous names Morgan le Fée, King Arthur's sister in Malory's *History of Prince Arthur*; Edward Morgan Forster, author of *A Room with a View* and *Howard's End*.

Morwenna (f)
Cornish and Welsh, from Celtic, meaning 'maiden'.
Famous name Saint Morwenna who gave her name to Morwenstowe on Cornwall's north coast.

Moses (m)
Biblical, meaning 'saviour'.

Mostyn (m)
Welsh, originally place name in Clwyd.

Murdoch (m)
Gaelic, meaning 'sea warrior'.

Muriel (f)
Of Celtic origin, meaning 'sea bright'.
Famous name Muriel Spark, Scottish novelist.

Murray (m)
Scottish, originally a surname based on a place, Moray.

Myfanwy (f)
Welsh, meaning 'woman'.

Myra (f)
Seventeenth-century invention, possibly an anagram of Mary; possibly from the Greek, meaning 'she who laments'.

Myrna (f)
Irish and English, based on Gaelic Muirne.
Famous name Myrna Loy, early film star.

Myron (m)
English, from Greek, meaning 'myrrh'.
Famous name Myron, Greek sculptor of the fifth century BC.

Myrtle (f)
Named after the plant. Ancient Jews believed myrtle leaves were a protection against witches. The name became popular in Victorian times.

N

Nadia (f)
English and French, of Russian origin.
Variants Nadya, Nadja.
Famous name Nadia Boulanger, French conductor and musician.

Nadine (f)
Russian, meaning 'hope'.
Variants Nadia, Nada.
Famous name Nadine Gordimer, South African novelist.

Nan (f)
Diminutive of Ann and Nancy.

Nancy (f)
Diminutive of Ann, used independently since the end of the eighteenth century.
Variants Nanci(e), Nance, Nanette.
Diminutive Nan.
Famous names Nancy Reagan, wife of former president,

Ronald Reagan; Nancy Mitford, English author renowned for her wit.

Nanette (f)
English, derived from Nan.
Famous name Nanette Newman, television actress.

Naomi (f)
Hebrew, meaning 'pleasantness'.
Variant Naomia.
Famous name Naomi Campbell, English supermodel, singer and author.

Nat (m)
See Nathan.

Natalie (f)
Latin, meaning 'the Lord's birth day'.
Variants Nathalie, Natalya, Natalee, Natelie, Natasha (diminutive Tasha) Natashia, Natacha, Noela (see Noel).
Famous name Natalie Wood, American actress.

Natasha (f)
Variation of Natalie.

Nathan (m)
Hebrew, meaning 'he has given'.

Nathaniel (m)
Hebrew, meaning 'God has given'.
Variant Nathanael.
Diminutives Nat, Natty.
Famous names Nat King Cole, renowned singer, pianist and actor; Nathaniel Hawthorne, American author of *The Scarlet Letter*.

Neal (m)
Variation of Neil.
Famous name Neal Ascherson, journalist.

Ned (m)
Diminutive of Edward and sometimes Edmund.
Famous name Ned Sherrin, author and broadcaster.

Neil (m)
From Gaelic Niall.
Variant Neal.
Famous name Neil Sedaka, American popular singer.

Nell (f)
English diminutive of Eleanor, Ellen and Helen used in its own right.
Diminutives Nellie, Nelly.
Famous names Nell Gwyn, mistress to Charles II; Nell Dunn, English novelist and playwright.

Nelson (m)
Surname, meaning 'son of Neil'.
Famous name Nelson Mandela, African nationalist leader and President of S. Africa.

Nerys (f)
Welsh, of fairly recent and uncertain origin.
Famous name Nerys Hughes, actress.

Nessa (f)
Diminutive of Vanessa and used in its own right. Also derives from Gaelic name Neassa.
Diminutives Ness, Nessie.

Nesta (f)
Welsh diminutive form of Agnes.

Netta (f)
Variation of Nettie.

Nettie (f)
Derived from names ending in 'nette', such as Annette.

Neville (m)
Norman surname, meaning 'new town'.
Variants Nevil, Nevile, Nevill.
Famous name Neville Shute, popular author.

Ngaio (f)
New Zealand name derived from a Maori word for certain tree.
Famous name Ngaio Marsh, crime writer.

Niall (m)
Irish and Scottish. Gaelic for Neil.

Nigel (m)
Latin form of Neil.
Diminutives Nidge, Nige.
Feminine Nigella.
Famous name Nigel Mansell, English motor racing driver and world champion in 1992.

Nicola (f)
Feminine of Nicholas.
Variants Nikola, Nicole, Nichole, Nicholette, Nicolette, Nicoletta, Nicol.
Diminutives Nicky, Nicki, Nikki, Niki, Nikky, Collette (from Nicollette).
Famous name Nicola Pagett, actress.

Nicholas (m)
Greek, comprised of 'victory' and 'people'.

Variants Nicolas, Nicol, Nickolas, Nichol, Nicholl, Nico.
Diminutives Nick, Nicki, Colin.
Famous names Nick Faldo, English golfer, the first Britain in 54 years to win three British Open titles.

Nikki (f)
Diminutive of Nicola, used in its own right.
Variants Nicki, Nicky, Nickie.

Nina (f)
Russian diminutive of Annina, Janina, Antonina.
Variants Ninette, Ninita, Ninetta.

Ninette (f)
Early twentieth-century diminutive of Nina.
Famous name Dame Ninette de Valois, ballet dancer.

Ninian (m)
Recent revival of old Scottish and Irish name the origin of which is not known.

Nita (f)
Diminutive of Anita.

Noel (m)
Old French, meaning 'Christmas'.
Feminine Noelle.
Famous name Noël Barber, BBC foreign correspondent and author.

Nolan (m)
Irish surname, meaning 'famous'.

Nolene (f)
Australian, based on Nolan.
Variant Noleen.

Nona (f)
Latin, meaning 'ninth'.

Norma (f)
See Norman.

Norman (m)
Old English, meaning 'northerner'.
Variant Norris.
Feminine Norma.
Diminutive Norrie.
Famous names Norman Wisdom, English actor and comedian; Norman Mailer, US writer; Norma Major, wife of British prime minister.

Nova (f)
Latin, meaning 'new'.

Nuala (f)
Irish diminutive of Gaelic Fionnuala, now used in its own right.

Nydia (f)
Possibly Latin, meaning 'nest'.

O

Oberon (m)
Variation of Auberon. In Shakespeare's *A Midsummer Night's Dream*, he is king of the fairies.

Octavia (f)
Latin, sister of the Roman Emperor Augustus and celebrated for her beauty.
Famous name Octavia Hill, founder of the National Trust.

Odette (f)
German, meaning 'riches'.
Variants Odella, Odelle, Odelyn, Odile.
Masculine Odell.
Famous name 'Odette', French Resistance fighter of the World War 2.

Olga (f)
Russian variation of Helga.
Diminutive Olya.

Olive (f)
Nineteenth-century name, based on plant – the olive branch was a sign of peace.

Olivia (f)
Latin, meaning 'olive'.
Variants Olive, Olivette.
Masculine Oliver, Olivier.
Diminutives Ollie, Livvy, Libby (see also Elizabeth).
Famous names Olivia de Havilland, American actress; Oliver Cromwell, Britsh statesman and soldier; Oliver Stone, American film director and screenwriter.

Ollie (m)
Diminutive of Oliver.

Olwen (f)
Welsh, meaning 'blessed'.

Oona (f)
Irish variation of Una.
Variants Oonagh, Una.

Ophelia (f)
Greek, meaning 'help'.

Orlando (m)
Italian for Roland, meaning 'famous land'.
Famous names Hero of the Charlemagne romances; title and main character of the novel by Virginia Woolf.

Orson (m)
Latin, meaning 'bear'.
Variant Orsino.
Feminine Ursula.
Famous name Orson Welles, American actor, screenwriter, director and producer.

Osbert (m)
Old English, meaning 'god and famous'.

Famous names Osbert Sitwell, writer; Osbert Lancaster, cartoonist.

Oscar (m)
Old English, meaning 'god-spear'.
Famous name Oscar Wilde, English novelist and playwright.

Oswald (m)
Victorian revival of Old English, meaning 'rule of God'.
Diminutive Oz.
Famous names Saint Oswald, King of Northumbria in the seventh century; Oswald Mosley, Fascist politician.

Otis (m)
American, derived from surname.
Famous name Otis Redding, American soul singer.

Owen (m)
Greek, meaning 'well-born'.
Variant Owain (Welsh).
Feminine Owena.

P

Paddy (m)
Diminutive of Patrick.
Famous name Paddy Ashdown, British politician.

Padraig (m)
Irish, Gaelic version of Patrick.
Variant Padraic.
Famous name Padraic Colum, Irish poet and playwright.

Paige (f)
Recent American invention from surname.

Pamela (f)
Name invented by Sir Philip Sidney in *The Arcadia.*
Variants Pamelia, Pamilia, Pamella, Pamila, Pammala.
Diminutive Pam (used independently).

Pandora (f)
English, from Greek, meaning 'all-gifted'. In mythology, she was the first mortal woman. Prometheus brought her a large box which she secretly opened and all the evils of the world flew out.

Pansy (f)
A Victorian flower name.

Pat (m,f)
Diminutive of Patricia and Patrick.
Variants Patty, Patti, Pattie.

Patience (f)
Seventeenth-century favourite, because of its meaning, which also included suffering.

Patricia (f)
Feminine of Patrick.
Variants Patrika, Patrishka, Patrice.
Diminutives Pat, Patsy, Patti, Patty, Tricia, Trisha.
Famous name Patricia Hodge, English actress.

Patrick (m)
Latin, meaning 'noble'.
Variants Padraig (Irish), Patric.
Diminutives Pat, Paddy.
Famous name Patrick Moore, television presnter and astronomer.

Patsy (f)
Diminutive of Patricia.

Paul (m)
Latin, meaning 'small'.
Variants Paolo (Italian), Pablo (Spanish).
Feminine Paula, Paulene, Paulette, Pauletta, Paulina, Paulann(e).
Famous names St Paul the Apostle; Paul 'Gazza' Gascoigne, English footballer; Paul Schofield, actor; Paul Newman, film actor.

Pearce (m)
English and Irish variation of Pierce and Piers.

Pearl (f)
Victorian name after semi-precious stone.

Peggy (f)
Diminutive of Margaret.
Diminutive Peg.

Penelope (f)
Greek, meaning 'a bobbin' or possibly a kind of bird.
Famous names Penelope, the wife of Ulysses; Penelope Keith, English actress.

Pepita (f)
Diminutive of Josefa, but used in its own right.

Percival (m)
Old French variation of Parzifal, and mentioned in Arthurian legend as the totally pure knight who alone would succeed in finding the Holy Grail.

Percy (m)
English surname, from Persius.
Famous names Percy Bysshe Shelley, Romantic poet; Percy Grainger, Australian composer and pianist.

Perdita (f)
Lain, meaning 'lost'.
Famous name Perdita, daughter of Hermione and Leontes in Shakespeare's *The Winter's Tale*.

Peregrine (m)
From Latin, meaning 'foreigner', hence 'pilgrim'. It is also a hawk.

Famous name Peregrine Worsthorne, journalist.

Perry (m)
Diminutive of Peregrine, Latin, meaning 'stranger'.
Famous names Perry Como, American singer and actor; Perry Mason, the fictional detective.

Pet (f)
Diminutive of Petula.

Peta (f)
Recent feminine variation of Peter.

Peter (m)
Greek, meaning 'stone'.
Variants Piers, Pearce, Pierce, Pedro, Pierre.
Diminutive Pete.
Feminine Peta, Petena, Petra, Petranella, Perterina, Petrina, Petrona, Petrice.
Famous names Pete Townshend, guitar and songwriter with 'The Who'; actors Peter Ustinov, Peter Sellers and Peter Finch.

Petula (f)
Recent English, origin unknown.
Diminutive Pet.
Famous name Petula Clark, popular singer.

Philip (m)
Greek, meaning 'love of horses'.
Variants Philipp, Philippe, Phillip.
Diminutives Phil, Pip, Flip, Fyl.
Feminine Philippa, Phillipa, Philipa.
Diminutive Pippa.
Famous name Phil Collins, singer/songwriter.

Philomena (f)
Greek, meaning 'beloved'.
Variants Philomene, Philomina, Filomena.

Phoebe (f)
Latin form of Greek, meaning 'brightness', name attributed to Diana, goddess of the moon.

Phyllis (f)
From Greek mythology, meaning 'foliage'.

Pia (f)
Popular Italian name, feminine of Pius, meaning 'pious'. Now used in English.

Pierce (m)
See Piers.

Piers (m)
Medieval English form of Peter, from Old French, appearing in the epic poem, *Piers Plowman* by William Langland, at that time.
Famous name Piers Paul Read, author.

Pip (m,f)
Diminutive of Philip and Philippa.

Pippa (f)
Diminutive of Philippa, but also used in its own right.
Famous name Robert Browning's poem, 'Pippa Passes'.

Polly (f)
Variant of Molly, now used in its own right.
Famous name Polly Devlin, journalist.

Poppy (f)
From the flower.

Famous name A character in Mary Wesley's novel, *The Vacillations of Poppy Carew.*

Portia (f)
From the Roman clan name.
Famous name Portia, the rich heiress in Shakespeare's comedy, *The Merchant of Venice.*

Posy (f)
Diminutive of Josephine, now used in its own right.
Famous name Posy Simmonds, of cartoon strip in the *Guardian.*

Price (m)
From the Welsh surname meaning 'son of Rhys'.
Variant Pryce.

Primrose (f)
Victorian name of early spring flower.

Priscilla (f)
Feminine diminutive of Prisca, a Roman Christian maiden tortured and beheaded under the Emperor Claudius II. This name was much used by the Puritans and is still in use.
Dinimutive Cilla.
Famous names Priscilla Presley, actress and wife of the late Elvis Presley, singer; Cilla Black (born White), pop singer and television hostess.

Prudence (f)
Word used as a name.
Diminutives Pru, Prue, Purdy.

Prunella (f)
Victorian invention made up of Latin *pruna*, meaning plum and -ella.
Diminutives Prue, Pru.
Famous name Prunella Scales, actress.

Q

Queenie (f)
Pet name derived from Regina, meaning 'queen'.

Quentin (m)
From St Quentin.
Variants Quintin, Quinton.
Feminine Quintina, Quinella, Quinetta.
Diminutives Quin, Quinn.

Quincy (m)
From the French place name.
Variants Quincey, Quintus.
Famous name John Quincy Adams, former President of the United States.

Quintus (m)
Roman, meaning 'fifth'.

R

Rachel (f)
Hebrew, meaning 'ewe'.
Variants Rachael, Racheal, Rachelle, Raquel.
Famous name Raquel Welch (born Tejada), film actress renowned for her beauty.

Raealene (f)
Recent Australian combination of Rae and -line.

Raisa (f)
Russian, from Greek name, Raisa, possibly meaning 'adaptable'. There was an early Christian martyr of this name.
Diminutive Raya.
Famous name Raisa Gorbachev, wife of the Soviet leader.

Ralph (m)
Old English, meaning 'wolf counsel'.
Variants Ralf, Rafe, Raoul.
Feminine Ralphina.
Diminutive Ralphie.
Famous name Ralph Steadman, cartoonist.

Ramona (f)
Spanish, having the same origin as Raymond, and meaning 'advice' and 'protector'.
Masculine Ramon.

Ramsay (m)
Scottish, originally a surname, meaning 'wild garlic' and 'island'. It was imported into Scotland from Huntingdonshire in the twelfth century, when the brother of King Alexander I was granted the earldom of Huntingdon.
Variant Ramsey.
Famous name Ramsey Macdonald, British prime minister.

Randall (m)
Medieval variation of Randolf.
Variants Randal, Randle, Randel, Randell.

Randolph (m)
Norman meaning 'shield edge' and 'wolf'.
Variants Randal, Randall, Randel, Ranulph.
Diminutives Randi, Randy.
Famous name Ranulph Fiennes, English polar explorer and author.

Randy (m,f)
Australian and American diminutive of Randolf, Andrew, Randall, and Miranda. Used in its own right by men, perhaps for the added glister of its meaning.

Ranulf (m)
Scottish from Old Norse, meaning 'advice' and 'wolf'.

Raoul (m)
French variant of Ralph.
Variant Raul.

Raphael (m)
An archangel's name, used in early Christian times.
Variant Rafael.
Feminine Raffaella.

Raquel (f)
See Rachel.

Ray (m)
Diminutive of Raymond, now used in its own right.
Famous name Ray Charles, popular blind singer.

Raymond (m)
Norman, meaning 'might, protection'.
Variants Raimond, Ramon, Raymund, Raimund.
Diminutive Ray (used independently).
Famous names Raymond Chandler, American crime writer; Ray Charles, American soul singer.

Rayner (m)
Norman, from Germanic, meaning 'advice' and 'warrior'.
Variants Rainer, Rainier.
Famous name Rayner Heppenstall, novelist.

Rebecca (f)
Hebrew, possibly meaning 'noose'.
Variants Rebeca, Rebeccah, Rebeckah, Rebekka (Greek).
Diminutives Rebbie, Becky.
Famous names Rebecca West, writer, feminist and author, H. G. Wells' lover; *Rebecca*, the novel by Daphne du Maurier.

Rees (m)
Welsh, anglicized version of Rhys.

Reg (m)
See Reginald.

Reggie (m)
See Reginald.

Reginald (m)
Old English, meaning 'power'.
Variant Ronald, Reynold.
Diminutives Ron, Reg, Reggie, Rex (used independently).

Rena (f)
Anglicized version of Renée of recent origin.
Variant Rina.

Renata (f)
Common in Italy and Germany, meaning 'reborn'.
Variant Renate.
Famous name Renata Tebaldi, Italian soprano.

René (m)
French, meaning 'reborn'.
Feminine René, Renee.
Famous name René Cutforth, journalist.

Reuben (m)
Hebrew name, meaning 'behold, a son'. Common in nineteenth century and still found in some country areas.
Variant Ruben.

Rex (m)
Latin, meaning 'king'.
Famous name Rex Harrison, actor.

Rhiannon (f)
Welsh, meaning 'nymph'.

Rhoda (f)
From Greek, meaning either 'rose' or 'a woman from Rhodes'. Rhoda appears in the New Testament in the house of Mary, mother of John.

Rhona (f)
Scottish, of unknown derivation, originating in Victorian times.

Rhys (m)
Welsh, meaning 'ardour'.

Richard (m)
Old German, meaning 'strong ruler'.
Variant Ricardo.
Feminine Ricarda.
Diminutives Rich, Hitch, Rick, Dick, Ricardo, Ricky, Richie, Ricki, Richey.
Famous names Dick Whittington, Lord Mayor of London; actors Richard Burton and Richard Attenborough; Rick Wakeman, American musician.

Ridley (m)
Originally a surname derived from a place name, of which there are many, meaning 'reeds and clearing'. The name was adopted by Christians after the burning at the stake of Bishop Nicholas Ridley in the sixteenth-century.

Rita (f)
English diminutive of Margarita, but used in its own right.
Famous name Rita Hayworth, film actress.

Roald (m)
Old Norse, meaning 'fame'.
Famous name Roald Dahl, much-loved English children's author.

Robert (m)
Old English, meaning 'fame' and 'bright'.
Feminine Roberta, Robertina.
Diminutives Bob, Bobby, Rob, Robbie, Robin, Robyn.
Famous names Robert Mitchum, American actor; Roberta Flack, American singer.

Robin (m,f)
Diminutive of Robert, used independently.
Diminutives Rob, Robbie.
Feminine Robin, Robyn, Robina.
Famous name Robin Williams, American comic actor.

Rocco (m)
Italian form of Old German, meaning 'repose'.
Variant Rocky.

Rocky (m)
Recent American, coined from a nickname.
Famous name Rocky Marciano, heavyweight boxing champion.

Rod (m)
See Rodney and Roderick.

Roderick (m)
Old German, meaning 'fame' aand 'rule'.
Variants Rodrick, Roderic, Rodric.
Diminutives Rod, Roddy, Rick.

Roger (m)
Old German, meaning 'fame' and 'spear'.

Variant Rodger.
Famous names Roger Moore, actor who played James Bond; Roger Vadim, French film actor and director.

Rodney (m)
English surname and place name.

Roland (m)
English and French, from Germanic, meaning 'fame' and 'territory', and introduced by the Normans. The name is recorded in the early French epic *The Song of Roland* (eighth century).
Variants Orlando, Rowland.
Feminine Rolande.

Rolf (m)
See Rudolph.

Rollo (m)
Latinized version of Rolf, which first appeared in Latin documents in medieval times. Recently revived.
Famous name Rollo May, psychologist and writer.

Romy (f)
Diminutive of Rosemary, but used in its own right.
Famous name Romy Schneider, film actress.

Ronald (m)
See Reginald.
Famous name Ronald Reagan, US president.

Ronnie (m)
See Ronald.

Rory (m)
Gaelic, meaning 'red'.

Ros (f)
See Rosalind and Rosamund.

Rosa (f)
Latinized version of Rose.

Rosabella (f)
Uncertain origin, meaning 'beautiful rose'.

Rosaleen (f)
See Rosalind.

Rosalie (f)
French variation of Rosalia. Saint Rosalia was a twelfth-century martyred virgin from Palermo.

Rosamund (f)
Latin, meaning 'rose of the world'.

Rosanne (f)
Of recent origin. A combination of Rose and Anne.
Variants Roseanne, Rosanna.

Rose (f)
This name was used extensively in medieval times.
Variant Rosa.
Diminutive Rosie.

Rosemary (f)
From the flowering herb.

Rosie (f)
Diminutive of all the 'Rose' names.

Ross (m)
Scottish surname and place name.

Rowan (m)
Irish, meaning 'red'.

Rowena (f)
Latinized version of Saxon name meaning 'fame' and 'joy'.
Variant Rhonwyn.

Roxana (f)
Persian, meaning 'dawn'.
Variants Roxenne, Roxanne, Roxianne.
Diminutives Roxie, Roxy.
Famous name Roxanne, the object of desire in Edmond Rosthand's novel, *Cyrano de Bergerac* (1897).

Roy (m)
Originally Scottish, being an anglicization of Gaelic, meaning 'red'. It may also be an anglicization of the French word for 'king'.
Famous names Roy Hattersley, Socialist politician; Roy Hudd, much loved actor; Roy Campbell, poet; Roy Lichtenstein, American pop artist.

Royston (m)
Originally a surname, derived from a place name. Of recent popularity in Britain.

Roz (f)
See Rosalind, Rosamund.
Variant Rozy.

Ruby (f)
A Victorian name taken from the red precious stone. Now out of fashion.

Rudolf (m)
English and northern European name, from the Germanic, meaning 'fame' and 'wolf'. It was a family name of the Habsburgs, Holy Roman Emperors.
Variant Rudolph.

Diminutive Rudi, Rudy.
Famous names Rudolph Valentino, film star and idol of the 1920s; Rudolph Nureyev, Russian ballet-dancer.

Rufus (m)
Latin, meaning 'red-haired'.

Rupert (m)
German form of Robert.
Famous name Rupert Murdoch, Australian newspaper magnate.

Russel (m)
French nickname 'Rousel', meaning 'little red one'.
Variant Russell.

Ruth (f)
Hebrew, possible meaning 'friendship'.
Famous names Ruth Prawer Jhabvala, novelist, best known for her 1975 Booker Prize-winning novel *Heat and Dust*.

Ryan (m)
American, Australian and Irish, from the Gaelic, meaning 'descendant of Rian', 'ri' probably meaning 'king'.

S

Sabina (f)
Latin, meaning 'Sabine woman'.
Variants Sabine, Sabrina, Sabre, Savina.
Diminutive Bina (used independently).

Sacha (m,f)
Diminutive of Alexander.
Feminine Sasha.

Sacheverell (m)
Of Norman origin, from a place name meaning 'deer leap', and coined as a baronial surname.
Diminutive Sachie.
Famous name Sir Sacheverell Sitwell, poet, art historian and travel writer.

Sadie (f)
Diminutive of Sarah, used independently.
Variant Saidee.

Saffron (f)
The colour and the flower (crocus).

Sagar (m)
Old English, meaning 'victory' and 'people'.

Sal (f)
See Sally.

Sally (f)
Diminutive of Sarah, used independently.
Variants Sallie, Salley, Sally Ann, Sally-Sann, Sallianne, Sallian.
Famous name Sally Gunnell, Olympic runner.

Salvador (m)
Spanish, meaning 'saviour'.
Variant Salvatore.
Famous name Salvador Dali, surrealist painter.

Sam (m,f)
See Samuel and Samantha.

Samantha (f)
Originated in American south in the eighteenth century, possibly a combination of Sam and Anthea.
Famous name Samantha Fox, model and singer.

Samuel (m)
From Hebrew, Shemuel, meaning 'asked for of God'. Samuel appears in the Bible as the son of Hannah. He established the Hebrew monarchy anointing both Saul and David. This is a popular Jewish name, also among nonconformists.
Diminutives Sam, Sammy.
Famous names Samuel Pepys, seventeenth-century diarist; Samuel Johnson, author and lexicographer; Samuel Butler, seventeenth-century satirist; Samuel Richardson, eighteenth-century novelist; Samuel Palmer, artist and visionary.

Sancha (f)
Latin, meaning 'holy'.
Variants Sanchia, Sancia.

Sandra (f)
See Alexandra.

Sandy (m,f)
See Alexander, Alexandra.

Sappho (f)
Greek lyric poet from the seventh century BC.

Sapphire (f)
Hebrew, meaning 'lapis lazuli'.

Sara (f)
See Sarah.

Sarah (f)
Hebrew, meaning 'princess'.
Variants Sara, Zara, Zarah, Saria, Sarina, Saritia, Zarita.
Famous names Sarah Bernhardt, famous nineteenth-century theatre actress.

Saskia (f)
Dutch, meaning 'Saxon'.
Famous name Saskia, the wife of Dutch artist Rembrandt.

Saul (m)
From the Hebrew, meaning 'prayed for'. Saul was one of the first kings of Israel. Both a Jewish and a Puritan name.
Famous name Saul Bellow, American novelist.

Savanna (f)
New name, meaning 'wild, grassy plain'.
Variants Savannah, Zavanna.

Scott (m)
English and Scottish, meaning 'a Scot'.
Variant Scot.
Famous name Francis Scott Fitzgerald, Jazz-Age writer.

Seamus (m)
Irish form of James.
Variants Seamas, Shamus.
Famous name Seamus Heaney, Irish Nobel prize-winning poet (1945).

Sean (m)
Irish form of John.
Variants Shaun, Shawn, Shane, Shayne.
Feminine Shauna, Sheena, Shiona, Shona, Shonagh, Shonah.
Famous names Sean O'Faolain, Irish short-story writer; Sean Connery, versatile film actor.

Sebastian (m)
Latin, meaning' man from Sebasta'.
Diminutive Seb.
Famous name Sebastian Coe, Olympic athlete and politician.

Selina (m)
From the name 'Selene', the goddess of the moon.
Variants Salena, Salina, Selinda, Celina.
Famous name Selina Scott, television newscaster.

Selma (f)
Possibly a contraction of Selina, mentioned in eighteenth-century writings; from the Arabic, meaning 'peace'.

Selwyn (m)
From an Old English name, meaning 'prosperity' and 'friend'.
Variant Selwin.
Famous name John Selwyn Gummer, British politician.

Seraphina (f)
Hebrew, meaning 'ardent'. The name derives from the order of angels, Seraphim, meaning 'burning ones'.
Variants Serafina.
Diminutive Fina.

Serena (f)
Latin, meaning 'serene, calm'.
Variants Serina, Serenah, Serenna.

Serge (m)
Roman family name.
Variants Sergio, Sergei.
Famous name Serge Lifar, Russian dancer.

Seth (m)
Hebrew, meaning 'appointed'.
Seth is an old English country name, still occasionally found. It was used in *Cold Comfort Farm*, Stella Gibbons' pastiche of D. H. Lawrence, and in *Emmerdale Farm*, television soap.

Seymour (m)
Norman aristocratic and place name.
Variants Seamor, Seamore, Seamour.

Shantel, Shantelle (f)
See Chantal.

Sharon (f)
Hebrew, meaning 'the plain'.
Variants Sharan, Sharen, Sharron, Sharone, Sharyn, Sharonda.
Diminutives Shari, Shara.
Famous name Sharon Stone, film actress.

Shavon(ne) (f)
See Siobhan.

Shawn (m)
American spelling of Sean.

Sheena (f)
Anglicization of Gaelic Sine, similar to Jane.
Famous name Sheena Macdonald, television journalist and presenter.

Sheila (f)
From Irish, Sile or Celia.
Variants Sheelagh, Shiela, Shelagh, Shayla.
Famous names Shelagh Delaney, playwright whose acclaimed first play, *A Taste of Honey* was written when she was just 17; Sheila Hancock, actress and comedienne.

Shelagh (f)
See Sheila.

Sheldon (m)
Based on place names in Devon, Derbyshire and Midlands.

Shelley (m,f)
Name derived from surname of Romantic poet.
Famous name Shelley Winters (born Shirley Schrift), American film actress.

Sheridan (m)
From the Irish surname.

Sherry, Sheri, Shereen, Shereena (f)
See Cher.

Sheryl (f)
See Cheryl.

Shevaun (f)
See Siobhan.

Shirley (f)
English place name meaning 'county' and 'clearing'.
Variants Sherlie, Shirlee, Shirleen.
Famous names Shirley Temple, child film star; Shirley Bassey, Welsh popular singer; Shirley Williams, former British Cabinet minister.

Sholto (m)
Gaelic, meaning 'sower'.

Shona (f)
Scottish, anglicized version of Gaelic Seonaid.

Shula (f)
From Hebrew meaning 'peacefulness'.
Famous name Shula Archer, in the BBC radio soap, *The Archers*.

Sian (f)
Welsh form of Jane.
Variants Shan, Shannon, Shana, Shannah, Shaneen, Shanida, Shanita, Shannel, Shanta.

Sibyl (f)
Latin, meaning 'a prophetess'.
Variants Sibella, Sibilla, Sibylla, Sybel, Sybella, Sybil.

Sidney (m)
Probably from Norman baronial surname, Saint-Denis.
Variant Sydney.
Diminutive Sid.
Famous names Sydney Smith, witty, early nineteenth-century essayist; Sidney Nolan, Australian painter; Sid Vicious, punk musician.

Sidonie (f)
Latin, meaning 'woman from Sidon'.
Variants Sidonia, Sidony, Sydonia.

Simon (m)
Greek, meaning 'snub nosed'.
Diminutives Sim, Simm.
Feminine Simone, Simona.
Famous names Simone de Beauvoir, French existentialist writer who wrote, *The Second Sex*; Simon Raven, English novelist; Simon Gray, Canadian dramatist.

Sinclair (m)
Probably from the Norman baronial name, Saint-Clair, and the name of a powerful Scottish highland clan.
Famous name Sinclair Lewis, American novelist.

Sinead (f)
Irish form of Janet.
Variant Seonaid.
Famous name Sinead O'Connor, controversial Irish singer.

Siobahn (f)
Irish form of Joan.
Variants Sioban, Siobhan, Shavon, Shevonne, Shivohn, Chavon, Chavonne, Chevonne.
Famous name Siobhan McKenna, actress.

Sissy (f)
See Cecilia.

Solange (f)
French, from Latin meaning 'solemn'.

Solly (m)
See Solomon.

Solomon (m)
Hebrew, meaning 'peace'.
Variant Soloman, Salman.
Diminutives Sol, Solly.
Feminine Salome.
Famous name Salman Rushdie, persecuted Booker Prize-winning novelist.

Sonia (f)
From the Russian diminutive of Sofya/Sophia. Popular in Britain since the 1920s.
Variants Sonya, Sonja.

Sophia (f)
Greek, meaning 'wisdom'.
Variants Sofia, Sonia (Russian), Sonya, Sonja (Scandanavian), Sophie (French), Sophy.
Diminutive Sophie.
Famous names Sophia Loren, Italian film actress; Sophie Tucker, American singer.

Sorcha (f)
Irish, meaning 'brightness'.

Sorrel (f)
Name derived from a plant with sour leaves, of fairly recent popularity.

Spencer (m)
Taken from an aristocratic surname.
Famous name Spencer Tracy, American film actor.

Spike (m)
Occasionally this nickname is given as a first name.
Famous names Spike Mays, East Anglian writer; Spike Milligan, much-loved comedian and writer.

Stacey (m,f)
From the surname, diminutive of Anastasia.
Variants Stacia, Staci(e), Stasia (also diminutives of Anastasia).

Stafford (m)
From aristocratic English surname.
Famous name Sir Stafford Cripps, politician who initiated post-war austerity programme in the 1940s and 1950s.

Stan (m)
See Stanley.

Stanley (m)
English place name, meaning 'stone clearing'. The name became popular as a result of Sir Henry Morton Stanley's fame as an explorer.
Variants Stanhope, Stanton.

Diminutive Stan.
Famous name Stanley Matthews, footballer.

Stella (f)
Sixteenth-century innovation, using the Latin for 'star'.
Variants Estelle, Estella.
Famous name Stella Gibbons, author of *Cold Comfort Farm.*

Stephen (m)
Greek, meaning 'crown'.
Variants Steven, Stevan, Stephan, Stephane, Stefan.
Diminutives Steve, Stevie.
Feminine Stephanie, Stefanie, Stephena.
Diminutives Steph, Stevie.
Famous names Stevie Wonder, American singer and songwriter; Stephane Grapelli, French jazz violinist; Steven Spielberg, film producer and director; Stephen Spender, poet; Stephanie Powers, film actress; Stevie Smith, American poet.

Steven (m)
See Stephen.

Stevie (f)
See Stephen.

St John (m)
After the saint, used since the middle of the nineteenth century.
Famous name Norman St John Stevas, British politician.

Storm (m)
Twentieth-century invention.
Famous name Storm Jamieson, thriller writer.

Stuart (m)
Old English, meaning 'keeper of the house'.
Variants Stewart, Steward.

Sukie (f)
See Susannah.

Sullivan (m)
Irish surname, meaning 'hawk-eyed'.

Susannah (f)
Hebrew, meaning 'lily'.
Variants Susan, Susanna, Suzanne, Suzette.
Diminutives Sue, Susey, Susie, Suzy, Suki, Sukey, Sukie.
Famous names Susannah York, English actress; Susan Sontag, American writer; Susan Hill, British novelist.

Susie (f)
See Susannah.

Sybil (f)
From the ancient Greek prophetess.
Variants Sibyl, Sibilla, Sybill, Sybille.
Famous name Dame Sybil Thorndike, English actress.

Sylvester, Silvester (m)
Latin, meaning 'rural'.
Famous name Sylvester Stallone, action hero film star.

Sylvia (f)
Italian and English, meaning 'wood'.
Variants Silvia, Silva.
Diminutive Sylvie.
Famous names Sylvia Plath, American poet and novelist; Sylvia Sims, actress.

T

Tabitha, Tabatha (f)
Aramaic, meaning 'gazelle'.

Talitha (f)
From Aramaic meaning 'little girl'. This name is found in the New Testament, and is occasionally used today.

Tallula (f)
This name has two distinct origins, one being American Indian (meaning unknown) and the other Irish Gaelic, meaning 'abundance' and 'princess'.
Variant (of Indian name) Tallulah.
Famous name Tallulah Bankhead, American film actress.

Tamar (f)
Modern name, from Hebrew meaning 'date palm'; Tamar appears in the Old Testament three times: in the Book of Genesis, as a daughter of King David, and also as a daughter of Absolom.

Tamara (f)
Russian, same Hebrew derivation as above.
Diminutive Tammy.
Famous name Tammy Wynette, American Country and Western singer.

Tanya (f)
From Tatious, King of the Sabines.
Variants Tatiana, Tana, Tanja, Tarnia.

Tara (f)
Irish, meaning 'hill'.
Made popular by the film, *Gone with the Wind*, in which the estate is named Tara.

Tarquin (m)
Named after the Roman emperors.
Famous name Tarquin Olivier, son of the actor Laurence Olivier.

Tasha (f)
See Natasha.

Tatiana (f)
See Tanya.

Taylor (m)
From the surname.

Teddy (m)
See Edward.

Terence (m)
From the Roman clan name.
Diminutive Terry.
Famous name Terence Stamp, English actor.

Teresa (f)
See Theresa.

Terri (f)
Modern American name, deriving from Terry.

Terry (m)
See Terence.

Tessa (f)
Originally a shortened form of Theresa, but now used in its own right.
Diminutive Tess.
Famous name Thomas Hardy's heroine Tess, in *Tess of the D'Urbervilles*.

Thea (f)
Diminutive of Dorothea, but often used in is own right.
Famous name Thea Porter, dress designer.

Thelma (f)
From the Greek meaning 'wish'. Became popular after the publication of Marie Gorelli's novel, *Thelma* in Victorian times.

Theo (m)
See Theodore.

Theodore (m)
From the Greek, meaning 'gift of God'.
Feminine Theodora.
Diminutive Theo.

Theresa (f)
Origin uncertain, but much used after the fame of Saint Therêse of Lisieux, who as a child had visions of the Virgin Mary.

Variants Therèse, Teresa.
Famous name Teresa Braganza, opera singer.

Thomas (m)
Aramaic, meaning 'twin'.
Diminutives Tom, Tommy.
Famous names Tommy Nutter, the trend-setting English tailor; Thomas Cook, founder of the travel company; Thomas Stearns Eliot, major American poet, of English adoption; Thomas Hardy, novelist; Thomas Keneally, Australian Booker prize-winning novelist; Tom Sharpe, comic novelist; Tommy Steele, pop singer; Thomas Hearns, boxer.

Thomasine (f)
Feminine of Thomas.
Variants Thomasena, Thomasina, Thomasin, Tamsin, Tamzin, Thomazin(e).
Diminutives Tammie, Tammy, Tami.

Tiffany (f)
Once a common name for girls born on the Feast of Epiphany. Became popular again, after the film, *Breakfast at Tiffany's* with its theme song, 'Moon River', in the early 1960s.

Tilly (f)
See Matilda.

Tim (m)
See Timothy.

Timothy (m)
Greek, meaning 'honour' and 'God'.
Diminutives Tim, Timmy.
Famous names Timothy West, actor; Timothy O'Leary, hippy guru.

Tina, Teena (f)
One shortened form of Christina, now much used in its own right.
Famous name Tina Turner, rock singer.

Tobias (m)
Hebrew, meaning 'God is good'. Made famous by the play *Tobias and the Angel*, based on the story in the Apocrypha.
Diminutive Toby.
Famous name Tobias Smollett, nineteenth-century novelist.

Toby (m)
See Tobias.

Todd (m)
Surname, meaning 'fox'.

Toni (f)
American abbreviation of Antonia, now sometimes used as a name in its own right.

Tony (m)
Diminutive of Anthony, used independently.
Feminine Toni, Tonia, Tonya, Tonja.

Torquil (m)
Scottish name, from Gaelic, Torcall.

Tracy (f)
From Greek, meaning 'carrying ears of corn', when it was a male name, but also from a contraction of Theresa. Now very popular, after the film *High Society* (1956), with heroine, Tracy Lord.
Variant Tracey.

Treena (f)
See Katherine.

Trelawney (m)
Cornish name, based on surname in John Hawkin's 'Song of the Western Men': 'And shall Trelawney live, and shall Trelawney die'.

Trevelyan (m)
Cornish name, based on place name, meaning 'place of Elian'.

Trevor (m)
From the Welsh surname meaning 'large settlement'.
Variant Trefor.

Tricia (f)
See Patricia.

Trina (f)
See Katherine.

Trisha (f)
See Patricia.

Tristan (m)
Of uncertain origin.
Variant Tristram.
Famous names The main character of the novel *Tristram Shandy* by Irish writer, Laurence Sterne; Wagner's opera *Tristan und Isolde*, based on the legend by Gotfried von Strassberg.

Trixie (f)
See Beatrice.

Troy (m)
Probably Norman, from the French place name.

Trudy (f)
Dimunitive of Gertrude, now used in its own right.
Variants Trudi, Trudie.

Truman (f)
American, but dating back to Old English, meaning 'trusty man'.
Variant Trueman.
Famous name Truman Capote, American writer.

Tyler (m)
From the surname.
Variant Tylar.

Tyrone (m)
American, from Irish county name.
Famous name Tyrone Power, American film actor.

U

Ulysses (m)
From the Latin name for the Greek hero, Odysses, who appears in Homer's *Odyssey*.
Variant Ulick (Irish).

Umberto (m)
Italian form of Humbert.
Famous name Umberto Eco, the Italian author who wrote *The Name of the Rose.*

Una (f)
Latin, meaning 'only'.
Variants Oona, Oonagh, Unity, Unita.
Famous names Una Stubbs, English actress; Oona O'Neill married Charlie Chaplin when she was 18 and he was 54.

Uriah (m)
Hebrew, meaning 'God is Light'.
Famous name The Charles Dickens' character, Uriah Heep, in the novel *David Copperfield*.

Ursula (f)
Latin, meaning 'she-bear'.

V

Valda (f)
Recent invention, an elaboration of Val.

Valentine (m)
Latin, meaning 'strong'.
Feminine Valentina, Valentia, Valerie.
Diminutive Val.
Famous name Valerie Hobson, English film actress.

Valerie (f)
From an old Roman name, meaning 'healthy'.

Vanessa (f)
Name invented by novelist Jonathan Swift for his lover, Esther Vanhomrigh.
Variant Vanetta.

Varda (f)
From Hebrew, meaning 'rose'.

Vaughan (m)
Welsh, surname meaning 'small'.
Variant Vaughn.
Famous name Ralph Vaughan Williams, composer.

Venetia (f)
From the Latin place name, Venice.

Vera (f)
Originally Russian, meaning 'faith', but popular in Britain since the 1900s.
Famous name Vera Brittain, writer, pacifist and feminist, known for her *Testament of Youth.*

Verity (f)
A Puritan name, from the Old French, meaning'truth'.
Famous name Verity Lambert, television film director.

Vernon (m)
Originally French baronial surname, from place name, meaning 'place of alders'.
Famous name Vernon Scannell, English poet.

Veronica (f)
Latin, meaning 'true image'. Veronica was the name given to the cloth, which, when wiped on Christ's face on his way to Calvary, retained his image in blood.
Variants Verona, Veron, Berenice, Bernice.

Veta (f)
Diminutive of Elizabeth.

Victor (m)
Latin, meaning 'conqueror, victor'.
Diminutive Vic.
Feminine Victoria, Victoire (French), Victorine.
Diminutives Vicki, Vicky.
Famous name Victor Hugo, French author and poet who wrote *Les Misérables* (1862); Queen Victoria who ruled in the nineteenth century for over sixty years;

Victoria Wood, comedienne; Victoria (known as Vita) Sackville-West, writer and gardener.

Vidal (m)
From Hebrew name, meaning 'life'.
Famous name Vidal Sassoon, hairdresser.

Vince (m)
See Vincent.

Vincent (m)
Latin, meaning 'conquering'.
Feminine Vincetta, Vincentia.
Famous name Vincent van Gogh, Dutch post-Impressionist painter.

Viola (f)
Latin form of Violet, the flower, and made famous by Shakespeare in *Twelfth Night*.

Violet (f)
From the flower.
Variants Viola, Violette, Violetta.
Famous name Violet Trefusis, the lover of novelist Vita Sackville-West.

Virginia (f)
Latin, meaning 'maiden'.
Diminutive Ginny.
Famous name, Virginia Woolf, English novelist and poet.

Vita (f)
Sanskrit, meaning 'wish, desire'.
Famous name Vita Sackville-West, English novelist.

Vivian (m,f)
Roman clan name, possibly meaning 'alive'.
Feminine variants Vivien, Vivienne, Vivianne.
Masculine variants Vyvian, Vyvyan.
Diminutive Viv.
Famous names Vivien Leigh, British actress; Viv Richards, West Indian cricketer.

W

Wade (m)
American, from surname, meaning 'ford'.

Wallace (m) **Wallis** (m,f)
Scottish and English, meaning 'a Welshman'.
Diminutive Wal, Wally.
Famous name Wallis Simpson, former Duchess of Windsor and wife of ex-King Edward VIII.

Wally (m)
See Wallace.

Walter (m)
Old German, meaning 'ruling clan'.
Diminutives Wally, Walt.
Famous names Walt Disney, famous filmmaker and animator; Walter Crane, children's illustrator; Walter de la Mare, distinguished poet.

Wanda (f)
Polish name of a fairytale princess, adopted by English.

Warren (m)
Recently popular name, derived from Norman place name, meaning 'game park'.
Famous name Warren Beatty, American film star.

Washington (m)
Surname and place name.
Diminutive Wash.

Wayne (m)
Recent coinage of what was a surname, meaning 'carter'. Its popularity is due to the American Western film actor, John Wayne (real name, Marion Michael Morrison).

Wendell (m)
From Old German, referring to a Slavonic tribe.
Famous name Oliver Wendell Holmes, nineteenth-century American writer.

Wendy (f)
Created by novelist J. M. Barrie in his children's book *Peter Pan* (1904).
Variants Wenda, Wendie.
Famous name Wendy Craig, British actress.

Wesley (m)
From the surname of the Wesley brothers, Charles and John, who founded the Methodist church, and still popular among Methodists.

Wilbur (m)
American, originating from a surname, meaning 'will' and 'fortress'.
Famous name Wilbur Smith, the popular novelist.

Wilfrid (m)
From Germanic, meaning, 'desire for peace'.
Variant Wilfred.
Diminutive Wilf, Wilfie, Wil.
Famous name Wilfred Owen, perhaps the greatest of all the First World War poets.

Will (m)
See William.

William (m)
Germanic name composed of 'will' and 'helmet'. One of the most popular of all English first names.
Variants Gwilym, Gwill (Welsh), Liam (Irish), Wilmot, Willis, Wilson.
Diminutives Will, Willie, Willy, Bill, Billy.
Feminine Wilma, Wilhemina, Williamina.
Diminutive Amina.
Famous names Bill Shankly, Scottish footballer and manager who once said 'Some people think football is a matter of life and death . . . I can assure them it is much more serious than that'; William the Conqueror, who led the Norman invasion into Britain in the eleventh century; William Shakespeare, best known of all English dramatists; William Wordsworth, most famous of the Romantic poets; William Walton, modern English composer; William Nicholson, early twentieth-century artist; Will Carling, Rugby football player; Prince William, second in line to the throne of England; Billy Graham, evangelist; Billy Connolly, Scottish comedian and entertainer.

Wilma (f)
Originally German feminine of William, but widely used in Britain.

Wilmer (m)
From Germanic, meaning 'famous will'.

Winifred (f)
Welsh, meaning 'holy reconciliation', or Old English, meaning 'joy and peace'.
Diminutives Freda, Frida, Frieda (see also Frederick), Winnie.

Winston (m)
From Old English name, meaning 'joy' and 'stone'.
Famous names Winston Spencer Churchill, politician, government leader during the World War 2, painter and writer; Winston Graham, novelist, famous for the 'Poldark' series.

X

Xanthe (f)
Greek, meaning 'yellow, golden'.

Xavier (m)
Spanish, meaning 'new house'.
Feminine Xaviera.
Variant Zavier.
Famous name St Francis Xavier, Spanish missionary.

Xenia (f)
Greek, meaning 'hospitality'.
Variants Zena, Zina, Zenia.

Xoán (m)
Galic form of John.
Variant Juan.

Y

Yale (m)
Surname meaning 'fertile hill'.

Yolanda (f)
Greek, meaning 'violet flower'.
Variants Yolande, Yalonda, Jolantha, Jolan, Yalinda, Iolanda, Iolanthe, Violante.
Diminutives Yola, Yolette.

Ysanne (f)
Combination of the names Isabel and Ann.

Yuri (m)
Russian form of George.
Variant Juri (Polish)
Famous name Yuri Geller, psychic.

Yves (m)
French, brought to Britain during the Norman Conquest.
Famous name Yves Saint Laurent, the French fashion designer.

Yvonne (f)
Feminine of Ivo, Ivon.
Variants Evette, Evonne, Evon, Yvette.

Z

Zachariah (m)
Hebrew, meaning 'God has remembered'.
Variants Zacariah, Zachary.
Diminutives Zac (pet form of Isaac, used independently), Zack.

Zandra (f)
See Alexandra.

Zara (f)
Twentieth-century version of Sarah.
Famous name Zara Phillips, daughter of Princess Anne.

Zelda (f)
Of uncertain origin, possibly from Yiddish name, meaning 'happiness'.
Famous name Zelda Fitzgerald, wife of the American writer, Francis Scott Fitzgerald.

Zeb (m)
Hebrew, shortened version of names, Zebuwn, meaning 'exaltation' and Zebedee, meaning 'my gift'.

Zillah (f)
Hebrew, meaning 'shade'.

Zipporah (f)
Hebrew, meaning 'bird'.

Zoe (f)
Greek, meaning 'life'.
Famous name Zoe Wanamaker, English actress.